FORERUNNERS: IDEAS FIRST FROM THE UNIVERSITY OF
MINNESOTA PRESS

Original e-works to spark new scholarship

FORERUNNERS: IDEAS FIRST is a thought-in-process series of break-
through digital works. Written between fresh ideas and finished books,
Forerunners draws on scholarly work initiated in notable blogs, social
media, conference plenaries, journal articles, and the synergy of academic exchange. This is gray literature publishing: where intense
thinking, change, and speculation take place in scholarship.

Ian Bogost
The Geek's Chihuahua: Living with Apple

Andrew Culp
Dark Deleuze

Grant Farred
Martin Heidegger Saved My Life

John Hartigan
Aesop's Anthropology: A Multispecies Approach

Mark Jarzombek
Digital Stockholm Syndrome in the Post-Ontological Age

Nicholas A. Knouf
How Noise Matters to Finance

Akira Mizuta Lippit
Cinema without Reflection: Jacques Derrida's Echopoiesis and Narcissism Adrift

Reinhold Martin
Mediators: Aesthetics, Politics, and the City

Shannon Mattern
Deep Mapping the Media City

Jussi Parikka
The Anthrobscene

Steven Shaviro
No Speed Limit: Three Essays on Accelerationism

Sharon Sliwinski
Mandela's Dark Years: A Political Theory of Dreaming

**Digital Stockholm Syndrome
in the Post-Ontological Age**

Digital Stockholm Syndrome in the Post-Ontological Age

Mark Jarzombek

University of Minnesota Press

MINNEAPOLIS

Published by the University of Minnesota Press
111 Third Avenue South, Suite 290
Minneapolis, MN 55401–2520
http://www.upress.umn.edu

Contents

Introduction

IMMANUEL KANT, writing at the end of the eighteenth century, defined the parameters of the modern sense of personhood by replacing the standard assumption of the superiority of the soul over the body with a more complex entanglement built around an innate sense of unity:

> No one is immediately conscious of a particular place in his body, but only the one that he as a human being occupies with respect to the world around him. . . . Where I feel, there I am. I am just as immediately in my fingertips as in my head. It is myself whose heel hurts and whose heart beats with emotion. When my corn aches, I feel the painful impression not in a brain nerve but at the end of my toe. . . . *My soul is wholly in my whole body and wholly in each of its parts.*[1]

So powerful was this claim that it remained a key element of nineteenth- and twentieth-century philosophy and was just as foundational to the dialectic of Hegel as it was to the psychohistoricism of Dilthey. It reached its most extreme figuration in Heidegger's claim that the original act of building, *bauen,* derived from nothing less—and nothing more!—than *Ich bin.* The claim also produced a vast symptomology to describe conditions that did not fit the mold—schizophrenia, mood disorders, psychosis, paranoia, bipolarism, and so on—all of which become "scientifically" verifiable proof in the negative of the more elusive existence of the modern notion of a stable and unified Self.

We are now in a situation where the discussion of ontology has to be updated. The world is *designed* from the macro to the micro/molecular level to fuse the algorithmic with the ontologi-

---

1. Gregory R. Johnson and Glen Alexander Magee, *Kant on Swedenborg: Dreams of a Spirit-Seer and Other Writings* (West Chester, Pa.: Swedenborg Foundation, 2002), emphasis original.

cal. The result is a digitally monitored, pharma-corrected, ontic-ecology now common to many people across the globe, not just the wealthy, and not just those savvy in the ways of the computer. The modern duality of the stable and the unstable when talking about the Self is increasingly revealed as little more than an artifice: a convenience.

This book is, however, not about the media/digital world of gaming and gadgets; nor is it about the geopolitics of globalization. It asks a more personal question, and tries to do so without first judging who we are or what we have now become. It used to be that we were what we believed, or we were what we ate. Now, we are determined by what data experts call our data exhaust—or, as I would like to call it, ontic exhaust. We participate in this exhaust making willingly and unwillingly, wittingly and unwittingly, purposefully and accidentally. The word *exhaust* is, of course, a misdirect. Unlike car exhaust that dissipates into the atmosphere, this exhaust is meticulously scrutinized, packaged, formatted, processed, sold, and resold to come back to us in the form of entertainment, social media, apps, health insurance, clickbait, data contracts, and the like.

Without this invisible ether of one and zeros, the world as we know it would, in fact, cease to function. It is the new oxygen, and everyone—and every *thing*—has to be dedicated to its production and maintenance. Unlike oxygen, which came into existence long before humans, this new substance is anthropocentric in that its production is a global/human enterprise. The individual, the corporation, the nation-state, and thousands of nameless hackers are increasingly shaping a destiny with an unknown proportion and an unknown termination date.

Though computers have been around for a while, this circulational condition has only emerged in the last five or so years, meaning that one has to completely rethink the philosophical and anthropological basis of our ontology and to do so without applying the lens of either victimhood or opportunity, the two modalities that are alien to this discussion. I do not, however, proclaim neutrality. Far from it. The questions are, What is this new ontology? What were the historical situations that produced it? And how do we adjust to the realities of our new Self? Only with these questions at least partially answered can we begin to develop a more substantial critique of the positional paradoxes that define the problem of Being.

1. Being-Global

GLOBAL WAS BORN in the age of aeronautics and Sputnik, with great circles wheeling around the planet bereft of topographical restrictions. *Global* back then implied something visceral about movement, maintained in the world of tourism, commerce, and overnight shipping. Increasingly, however, *global* has become a parasitic adjective: global industries, global science, global news, global education, global exchange, global warming, global imperialism, global war on terror, global markets, global jihadism, global integration, and so on. How many globals can a person comprehend? We live in a globalized world of global globalism.

All these globals are the noisy symptom of an otherwise relatively quiet transformation that has taken place. For there is another global in all of this for which the word *global* does not, however, appear. It is the "I" made global not by how much the I travels or where its clothes are made, and not necessarily by the fact that the I owns an iPhone or iPad, but by a universe of anonymously implemented firmwares, softwares, trackwares, ransomwares, trialwares, malwares, piratewares, and sharewares. The intermediaries are the satellites hovering above the planet. They are what make us global—what make *me* global.

Is there some way to reflect on this positioning/depositioning as a question of Being?

At first, it might seem that we should focus on someone who is savvy about emerging technologies, digital media, and a so-called culture of connectivity. Perhaps this is a person who travels a lot, a businessperson who understands to some degree the necessity, if not the logic, of capital, reads from his or her tablet, and worries about the next Global Crisis. A Hilton Cosmopolitan. Liberals would hope that this person is sensitive to the economic exploitation of capital. Conservatives would hope that this person enjoys making money. It doesn't matter. There is more to it than that. We see in the last years a new ontology, one that is not the classic Being-in-the-World (Plato and Buddha), not the modernist Being-in-the-World (Hegel, Nietzsche, and Heidegger), not the techno-liberated-performative cyborg of the 1990s, and not just a member of Facebook Universe. It is a new creature altogether—a new Being.

Without getting too complicated, let's say that the word Being points to life, to our social constructions, and to a sense of identity in the world, whether valid or not, whether validated or not. Needless to say, most philosophy, whether Eastern or Western, has tried to mold Being in a particular way. All philosophy operates on Being. Being is constructed *by* philosophy to be vulnerable to the operations *of* philosophy. As a result, Being is continuously told what to do, what to eat, how to work, how to behave, how to think, how to have sex, if at all, and, inevitably, how to think of oneself as superior.

So much for the past! Being today is moving on. It is far from seeking liberation. There is no liberation.

Ontology is always an opening—an opening for itself, an opening for others to poke around in. The new ontology may not realize—or even want to realize—that it is part of this give-and-take. But what is given and what is taken?

Not a global Being, but a Being-Global.

The first word points to an ontological fixity—or at least the artifice or aspiration for fixity, a worldview born for the most part in the agrocivilizational mind-set—and the second word to a deontological anywhere, born for the most part in a world of airplanes, ships, electronics, and PowerBars. Global strips Being of the arrogant presumption of *locus vivendi* and its associated set of reinforcements in culture and politics. That is the only purpose of the word *Global*: to offset the DNA of onto-centrism. Being and Global are now locked into each other in an antonymous relationship. Being-Global is like a positive and negative in a battery. The two sides test, modify, and produce each other's limits.

Being-Global is not a here and now but a here and now, here and not now, not here and now, not here and not now.

We travel with the flick of a wrist, with the rotation of our head, or with the movement of our retina. And everywhere we go, there are those who watch us, who go with us, who accompany us on our great digital journeys, like silent ghosts, the haunting, swirling algorithms of corporations, nations, police, hackers, and worse.

In the world of Being-Global, monotheism is dead.

The gods in the new pantheon have names, some familiar, some not, like Google, NSA, Cyber Caliphates, Baidu, Yandex, HSBC, AIG, Kmart, ExxonMobil, Coca-Cola Company, Grupo ACS, Holcim, Industrial and Commercial Bank of China—all augmented by a host of lesser gods who control shipping, steel, corn, movies, gasoline, and copyrights, down to the level of my DNA and protein consumption. Like most gods, they are known but remote, real but disembodied, reachable and yet abstract. They form a gaseous star producing a great, global combustion, shooting out a solar flare here and there to make things interesting but otherwise impeachable in their authority.

The great religions of the past put god in a house, a temple, a naos. But in even earlier days, gods—often in the form of animals and birds—moved about more freely. One could encounter them almost anywhere. They were luminous *and* dark, real *and* abstract, benevolent *and* violent—but, above all, they were a set of beings whose realities intertwined with the realities of the human world, whether in life or in dreams. They once lived globally on mountains or in trees; now they live globally in boardrooms, Internet cafés, and coat pockets. Their world is not static or sovereign like that of the traditional monotheistic deities. Our new gods marry, murder, flirt, propagate, go to war, and make peace. These ever-energetic gods are locked in vast, largely invisible struggles of warriors and demons, of victors and victims. Power and Substance are continually being exchanged through the digital ether that nourishes them.

2. Onto-Formation

I AM NOT INTERESTED in rehearsing the history of technology and its supposed advances. It is not computation that changed the status of Being but a series of different, partially related events that blended, added up, fused—conspired—to form the potential for something bigger: *complex system analysis + algorithmic mathematics + geosyncronicity + microprocessors + super-computers + location technology*. Added up, they produced a geopolitics of power that needed to be fed one thing: data. And what better data producers than the human? There are so many. This means that the more mobile we are and the smaller, cheaper, and more lightweight computers become—the more we can make the things of the world mobile/traceable—the better it is for the system. The *geosyncronic-algorithmic* world is a heat-seeking/heat-producing system. Heat is generated by motion (things, bodies, data).

How does one activate—illuminate/warm up—a population? How does one transform a mass of old-school (cold), organic creatures—that is, humans—into a new-school (hot) fog of data points?

Though the catchphrase in the United States is commercialization, the true genius of the United States—good or bad—is *civilianization*. Transferring military technology to commercial use required not just a certain type of political will but, more importantly, the creation of an ethos in which people see themselves differently, see technology differently. They have to see/think/feel as free from the specter of technology and its resident Cold War evils. Technology not only had to be rebranded and softened, it had to be rendered as living.

We have to understand what the word *natural* means as used by James Lingerfelt, who served as a senior consultant with IBM's

Global Smarter Cities Team. "The emergence of Big Data has become the newest natural resource of law enforcement."[1] Just because Lingerfelt has no clue about the geopolitical philosophy hidden in his bland statement does not mean that it is any less poignant.

But we should not immediately fall into some anxiety about Big Brother. The fundamental question is, What then happens when technology *disappears* into the human world? To understand that, we have to get from the military world to the world of the human. Back in the late 1970s, Mark Duchaineau, a well-known hacker, said that without a computer, "it would be like you didn't have your sight, or hearing. The computer is another sense or part of your being."[2] Today, a sentiment once known to a handful of computer geeks has become—or is becoming—the new normal. A Google executive stated it pretty well: "Google's goal is to become like breathing; just a necessary function for accomplishing what you need to do. You don't think about it, you don't really talk about it; you just instinctively do it."[3] We have to work backward from that thought to bring out its hidden implications.

What, then, does it mean when something once called technology, visible and palpable in the world in the form of machines, sounds, and sights—a trope of the processes of modernity and modernization—appears/disappears into the interiority *and* exteriority of Being?

The word *technology* is now meaningless, the residue of an anthrocentric worldview of Man and Tool and the elusive promise of *technē*. Technology has morphed into a bio-chemo-techno-spiritual-corporate environment that feeds the Human its sense-of-Self. We are at the beginning of a new history.

In looking backward on how this came to be, one should not isolate a single historical trajectory. There are multiple potential "be-

1. Doug Wyllie, "How 'Big Data' Is Helping Law Enforcement," PoliceOne, August 20, 2013, http://www.policeone.com/police-products /software/Data-Information-Sharing-Software/articles/6396543-How -Big-Data-is-helping-law-enforcement. Please note that unless otherwise indicated, all websites were verified as active as of August 10, 2015.

2. Steven Levy, *Hacker, Heroes of the Computer Revolution* (New York: Anchor Press, 1984), 378.

3. "The Genius of Google's Invisibility," VoiceGlance, January 21, 2015, http://voiceglance.com/the-genius-of-googles-invisibility.

ginning points," each associated with different types of temporalities and different types of energies. One of these points, for example, is the book *Industrial Dynamics,* written by Jay Wright Forrester, who taught at the MIT Sloan School of Management. The book is not about humans, however, but about industrial business cycles.

Forrester wanted to replace the word management with management laboratory,[4] but the full impact of the principle was held back, even for him, by the still old-fashioned notion of science as something that could take the dynamics out of dynamic situations: "management is in transition from an art, based only on experience, to a profession, based on an underlying structure of principles and science."[5] This argument opened a flood of research that marked the arrival of cybernetics, a transdisciplinary approach for exploring regulatory systems. In 1962, William Ross Ashby wrote *Introduction to Cybernetics.* The book deals primarily with homeostatic processes under the assumption that the brain is designed in this manner, though on a grand scale. Homeostasis is the property of a system in which variables are regulated so that internal conditions remain stable and relatively constant. Examples in the technical world include the thermostat, cruise control, and autopilot. Though many in government and business hoped that humans could be understood in this way, it soon became clear that the human is *not* a homeostatic organism.

Forrester made a second and more prescient argument: "physical systems, natural systems, and human systems are fundamentally of the same kind. . . . They differ primarily in their degree of complexity."[6] Today, we know that his statement needs to be slightly rewritten. These systems do *not* differ in terms of their complexity.

THE FIRST LAW OF POST-ONTOLOGICAL THERMODYNAMICS
The physical system (of data) = natural system = human system.

---

4. Jay W. Forrester, *Industrial Dynamics* (Cambridge, Mass.: MIT Press, 1961), 1.

5. Ibid.

6. Jay W. Forrester, "System Dynamics and the Lessons of 35 Years," in *A Systems-Based Approach to Policy Making,* ed. Kenyon B. De Greene (New York: Springer Science and Business Media, 1991), 202.

This is the first of three laws, of course. It took forty years for it to become the new normal.

A Brief Background

After World War II, the U.S. government, private endowments, and various corporations paid the RAND Corporation to inform policy makers on a wide variety of issues. One question that RAND addressed was, How does impersonal data produce an image of the human being? That, as it turned out, was the right question. If one starts with a "raw data set," based on information from the "real world," as one of RAND's theorists explained, how, then, does one describe that "world" and our "knowledge" of it without having to invoke some predetermined conceptualization or model that stands apart from the data?[7] For the answer, RAND proposed that models be measured not with respect to their ability to define certain objectives but with respect to how they produce *new* goals based on the principle of variables.

Models are measured not in terms of accuracy but in terms of effectiveness.

The project that asked these questions was given the code word Delphi.

It is thought that the name *delphoi* comes from the same root as δελφύς, *delphys* (womb), and may indicate archaic veneration of Gaia, the mother earth goddess, at Delphi, Greece, the site of the famous oracle in the Temple of Apollo. The gods have spoken.

Delphi analysts made diagrams, not equations. But soon there were equations to back it up—not just any old equations but algorithms, a mathematical procedure that solves a problem not once but n number of times. For centuries, algorithms took a backseat to calculus, which made it possible to determine the rate of change of distance compared to the time for objects moving at varying speeds. Classical mechanics, as it is known today, could predict the location of planets, meteors, and balls falling from the tower of Pisa. These laws, like those of ontology, were treated as first principles. They were particularly good at tracking cannon balls

---

7. Harold A. Linstone and Murray Turoff, "The Delphi Method," http://is.njit.edu/pubs/delphibook/ch1.html.

and then missiles.[8] Today: not variables but double variables; not missiles but cruise missiles; not cannon balls but UPS packages.

It started with the math genius Ada Lovelace (1815–52), the only child of the poet Lord Byron and Anne Isabella Byron. Between 1842 and 1843, she translated an article by Italian military engineer Luigi Menabrea on Charles Babbage's "analytic engine," at the end of which she added her own notes. They contain what many consider to be the first computer program—that is, an algorithm designed for a machine to carry out. It was not a real machine but, as she herself expressed it, "a new, a vast, and a powerful language . . . developed for the future use of analysis, in which to wield its truths so that these may become of more speedy and accurate practical application for the purposes of mankind than the means hitherto in our possession have rendered possible."[9]

Fast-forward to the 1970s. Put Delphi diagrams together with algorithmically charged computers and you get a new intelligentsia: knowledge prognosticators. They used words like PERT/CPM (developed by the U.S. Navy), SOON, morphological analysis, BRAILLE, and "relevance trees."

1980: The U.S. Department of Defense creates a computer nicknamed "Ada" (after Ada Lovelace). Its language is called MIL-STD-1815, reflecting the year of her birth. The fly-by-wire system software in the Boeing 777 is written in Ada. The Canadian Automated Air Traffic System also uses Ada to some extent, as does the United Kingdom's next-generation Interim Future Area Control Tools Support (iFACTS). Ada still lives!

1983: In 1971, Rene K. Pardo and Remy Landau patent an automatic natural order recalculation algorithm for spreadsheets (US 4398249). The U.S. Patent Office rejects the algorithm as being "a purely mathematical invention." However, in 1983, after twelve years of appeals, Pardo and Landau win: the court overturns the Patent Office's decision, establishing that, indeed, "something does not cease to become patentable merely because the point of

8. I use the word *algorithm* somewhat loosely and inclusively to include defaults, protocols, program interfaces, and the like.

9. L. F. Menabrea, "Sketch of the Analytical Engine Invented by Charles Babbage," *Bibliothèque Universelle de Genève* 82 (October 1842), http://www.fourmilab.ch/babbage/sketch.html.

novelty is in an algorithm."[10] This seemingly insignificant legal decision changes the future of humanity, for it was one of the first of several steps of the process of civilianization. Soon the race was on to patent all sorts of algorithms. It was the birth of Algorithm-Based Capitalism.

What if algorithms can study humans as opposed to missiles or business cycles? For that to happen, there needs to be systems that can first find humans and, second, transform them into data producers. And so the story begins again,

1945: The German inventor Christian Hülsmeyer, in 1904, demonstrated the feasibility of detecting a ship in dense fog. He called his detection device a "telemobiloscope." We today call it "radar." Can one find things from outer space? This was first proposed by the scientist and fiction writer Arthur C. Clarke back in 1945. In a paper called "Extra-Terrestrial Relays: Can Rocket Stations Give Worldwide Radio Coverage?," he wrote,

> Many may consider the solution proposed in this discussion too farfetched to be taken very seriously. It will be observed that one orbit, with a radius of 42,000 km, has a period of exactly 24 hours. A body in such an orbit, if its plane coincided with that of the earth's equator, would revolve with the earth and would thus be stationary above the same spot on the planet. It would remain fixed in the sky of a whole hemisphere and unlike all other heavenly bodies would neither rise nor set.[11]

Arthur Clarke imagined it, and Harold Rosen, an engineer at Hughes Aircraft Company, built it. Not only was the task technically difficult but he was also fighting many of the nation's top experts, who did not believe the idea would work. Even the boss, the eccentric billionaire Howard Hughes, was not sure the project was worth the modest investment.

1963–64: Rosen and his team develop the first operational geosynchronous satellite, Syncom 2, launched in 1963. They launched Syncom 3 in 1964 and used it to telecast the 1964 Summer

10. Court case quoted in "Novelty: Invention and Patent Law," http://lawi.us.

11. Arthur C. Clarke, "Extra-Terrestrial Relays: Can Rocket Stations Give World-Wide Radio Coverage?," *Wireless World*, October 1945, http://lakdiva.org/clarke/1945ww/1945ww_oct_305-308.html.

Olympics in Tokyo to the United States—the first television program to cross the Pacific Ocean. But the satellite's real use was military. In 1964, the U.S. Army, needing to coordinate its positioning of submarines and aircraft, orbits its first Sequential Collation of Range satellite used for geodetic surveying.

1984: Commercial Space Launch Act.

1991: Although military aircraft had used GPS for more than ten years—they were top secret and used mainly for submarines to get an accurate fix on their positions before they launched their submarine-launched ballistic missiles (SLBMs)—the system is still unknown even to much of the army. With a large-scale operation against Iraq on the horizon, U.S. Army commanders realize the need to supply frontline units with GPS devices. The problem is the limited number of devices on hand. In an October 1991 newsletter, the Center for Army Lessons Learned noted that at the outset of Operation Desert Shield, the army owned only five demonstration receivers, placed mainly on armored personnel carriers and food supply trucks. From then on, the military invests heavily in GPS.

2000: On May 1, President Clinton turns off the restricted availability of the GPS to the military. Over the next decade, the United States implements improvements to GPS service, including new signals for civil use and increased accuracy.

Today, hovering over the earth are approximately 140 geosynchronous satellites and an even larger number of orbiting satellites. Our lifelines to ourselves.

We are children of the gods of geosyncronicity.

However, to be fully civilianized: algorithmic modeling + global positioning needs *human scaling*:

1971: Intel 404. Though the processing revolution began in the 1960s in the context of space exploration, Intel 4004 is the first commercially successful microprocessor. It makes possible the first laptops; developed by aerospace engineers, they weighed twenty pounds!

1991: The Apple PowerBook series, with room for a palm rest and the inclusion of a pointing device (a trackball), sets the stage for the modern computer. It brings the human body into consideration. The rest we are familiar with.

1996: Enter JavaScript, developed by Brendan Eich while working for Netscape Communications Corporation. Java provides an environment in which "applets" can be run, appealing to nonprofessional programmers.[12] Though developed under the name "Mocha," the language is officially called "LiveScript" when it is first shipped in beta releases of Netscape Navigator 2.0 in September 1995. It was renamed "JavaScript" when it was deployed in Netscape browser version 2.0B3. JavaScript is a trademark of Oracle Corporation.[13] What began at Delphi found its resolution at Oracle.

However, to be fully civilianized, algorithmic modeling + global positioning + human scaling needs *speed*:

1985: The European Centre for Medium-Range Weather Forecasts, an independent intergovernmental organization supported by twenty-one European member states and thirteen cooperating states, goes into operation. Its headquarters in Reading, England, hosts one of the world's fastest supercomputers.[14]

1989: A new generation of supercomputers is launched; known as SX-3, they are developed by NEC Corporation in Japan.

1993: E-mail; Short Message Service (SMS).

1998: In *Working Knowledge,* Davenport and Prusak describe how knowledge is affected by the speed with which it moves through the organization (what they call "velocity") and the richness of how much context it has ("viscosity"): space dynamics and fluid dynamics combined. The authors give as an example a problem encountered by Mobil oil company engineers in the 1990s. Though they developed a new technique to improve drilling, which could produce huge savings (velocity), when they sent the memo out, nothing happened. The memo was too slow (a high level of viscosity) and an ineffective mode of communication. Mobil had to devise more direct ways to communicate with the drilling rigs.

2004: The chip-scaled atomic clock is unveiled. It allows for the synchronization of GPS devices the world over.

12. An applet is a small application that performs one specific task that runs within the scope of a dedicated widget engine or a larger program, often as a plug-in.

13. Charles Severance, "JavaScript: Designing a Language in 10 Days," *IEEE Computer Society* 45, no. 2 (2012): 7–8, http://www.computer.org/csdl /mags/co/2012/02/mco2012020007-abs.html; Mary Bellis, "The History of JavaScript," http://inventors.about.com/od/jstartinventions/a/JavaScript.htm.

14. Wikipedia, s.v. "European Centre for Medium-Range Weather Forecasts," http://en.wikipedia.org/wiki/European_Centre_for_Medium-Range _Weather_Forecasts.

2007: Google begins pumping more than $2 billion per quarter into its data center construction program. It designs a unique system based on modular units (the size of shipping containers) that can be constructed and moved to any location and assembled in groups (U.S. Patent 7278273).

Today: Stock exchanges can execute trades in under half a millionth of a second. Sophisticated algorithms battle for fractions of a cent. All of this is designed by a special breed of human algorithm designer known as a quants (quantitative analyst).[15] "Align yourself with the right kind of quant," reads the headline in a 2013 issue of *Harvard Business Review.*[16]

And finally: algorithmic modeling + global positioning + human scaling + computational speed = **data geopolitics.**

Political power used to be measured in missiles and submarines and the production of iron and silicon chips. Today there is a new geopolitical force: Data Management. Titan (yet another deity), built in the United States in 2014, is now the second-fastest supercomputer in the world. The largest is in China. Who, then, can control the economy-of-digital-capacity to outdo the United States and China? Having the tallest skyscraper was once an indicator of national pride; it is now Digital Density. "Governments and business leaders can now measure and manage digital strategies to take advantage of this opportunity, to more effectively compete."[17] Finland advertises its lack of restrictions; the euphemism is "data friendly." Canada claims that its cold weather makes for "greener" server farms. The cold climate is a supposedly natural way to reduce the heat output of the computers:

> Build your next data center in Finland: Finland is probably the data-friendliest country in Europe. Why? Node-point connectivity

15. Harry Markowitz's 1952 PhD thesis "Portfolio Selection" and its published version composed one of the first efforts in economic journals to formally adapt mathematical concepts to finance.

16. Thomas H. Davenport, "Keep Up with Your Quants," *Harvard Business Review,* July–August 2013, https://hbr.org/2013/07/keep-up-with-your-quants.

17. "Digital Density Index: Guiding Digital Transformation," Accenture Careers, http://www.accenture.com/us-en/landing-pages/Pages/digital-density -index-ad.aspx.

between West and East. Super-reliable power grid and infrastructure. Game-changing IT sector and attractive support packages. And that's just starters![18]

When it comes to building large-scale public cloud computing environments, Canada has a few unique advantages. Our country offers privacy and security legislations that meet international muster and we already have mature, high-speed networks. But there's one other asset that works in Canada's favour that may be less immediately obvious, but is a simple reality for every Canadian, particularly at this time of year. Put simply: We have cold. Lots and lots and lots of cold.[19]

The old geopolitics of nations and citizens, and of military and resources, is obsolete. The new equation is algorithmic modeling + global positioning + human scaling + computational speed + data geopolitics = Being-Global. Governments, banks, Google, and hackers all "play" with this equation.

18. "Build Your Next Data Center in Finland," Invest in Finland, http://www.investinfinland.fi/datacenter/main.php.

19. Robert Dutt, "Cold Front: Can Canada Play a Leading Role in the Cloud?," ChannelbuzzCA, December 8, 2010, http://www.channelbuzz.ca/2010/12/cold-front-can-canada-play-a-leading-role-in-the-cloud-846.

3. Post-Ontological

GLOBALIZATION IS TOO AMORPHOUS A TERM—and too saturated with old-fashioned, ideological presuppositions—to be of any use in this conversation. Furthermore, whereas globalization is thought to have emerged in the 1980s in the context of multinational corporations, the history of the globalized "I" only began to come into focus around 2005, after a two-decade warming-up period in which civilianization, deregulation, and population boom served as the three main catalysts. But the resultant, Big Volume Capitalism, would never have succeeded without the accompanying algorithmic revolution.

Let me rehearse the dates as they might have already slipped into our collective unconscious:

1978: Airline Deregulation Act

1980: Depository Institutions Deregulation and Monetary Control Act

1980: Motor Carrier Act

1980: Staggers Rail Act

1980: World population: 4.4 billion

1980: Ada (algorithm software designed by the U.S. Department of Defense)

1983: The civilianization of the algorithm for spreadsheets

1983: 33 percent of supermarkets have product scanners

1983: Home banking: Bank of America

1984: The civilianization of space (Commercial Space Launch Act of 1984)

1989: Fall of the Berlin Wall

1991: The civilianization of the World Wide Web

1991: The civilianization of the laptop: PowerBook

1992: National Energy Policy Act

1992: UPS ground tracking

1993: *Marketing Mapping: How to Use Revolutionary New Software to Find, Analyze, and Keep Customers*

1993: CERN (European Center for Nuclear Research) places World Wide Web in public domain

1994: MetaCrawler (one of the Web's first search engines)

1996: Telecommunications Act

1997: The first use of OnStar tracking for luxury cars

1999: Gramm–Leach–Bliley Act

2000: The civilianization of GPS

The moment has arrived:

2000: World population: 6.0 billion
2001: Wikipedia
2001: Google Earth
2001: iTunes

The birth of the so-called Social Media Age:

2003: Myspace
2004: Facebook
2004: Google Books
2005: YouTube
2006: Twitter
2014: Face detection in a portable camera[1]
2015: World population: 7.3 billion

Deregulation may have had its origins in a certain type of political vision (for better or worse), but it had, more importantly, two side effects that no one anticipated: first, the volumification of information, and second, the need to predict future trends.

The Being-Global world is population-centric. That is where the millions are made—made by the millions.

A billion new customers every ten years! An excellent business model.

---

1. Samsung Electronics Co., Ltd., "Apparatus, Medium, and Method for Photographing Based on Face Detection," December 29, 2010, http://patents .justia.com/patent/8891953.

The result of deregulation did not mean the end of regulation but rather the need to regulate in a whole different way. One did not create a series of commands posted on the door: "Do this, don't do that. The penalty is . . ." Those come from the traditional ontological point of view. The newly regulated human exits in an osmotic balance between what the system "sees" (data) and what the human "produces" (i.e., ontic information). There are no apparent don'ts; there are only dos; the system appears free (in the sense of unencumbered), thus making it attractive to the sense-of-Self and the illusion of opportunity. This constituted one of the greatest revisions of moral sensibilities since the dawn of civilization!

> Net-neutrality, AKA the internet, is like a giant sex party where everyone can have sex with anyone they want.
> —A NAKED PORN STAR making a pitch for net neutrality

The civilianization of the Self happened often legally, but just as often illegally, to the "embarrassment" of the powers that be. Techniques first developed for the military, the cyberweapon Stuxnet, for example, ended up in a form of criminal malware.[2] So why parse the difference between the legal and illegal? Stuxnet, after all, was used by the United States to hack Iranian computers.

The civilianization of the Self does not mean that there are no strings attached. On the contrary, the whole point is to attach strings. First, there are the strings to capital, then the strings—even further upstream—to the military-industrial complex (where it started), all bound together in a spaghetti soup of obligations, real *and* fictive, enforced *and* unenforceable, productive *and* antiproductive.

The modern-day Being-Global, using instruments cleansed of their overt military status, lives with a whole new understanding of capitalism and its role in society. The porosity is extreme. Behind the scenes, capitalism needs to militarize itself to protect itself against assault from corporations, governments, and hackers. The battles are violent, fierce, and, for the most part, inaudible to us mortals. The militarization of capitalism—boardrooms as war rooms—passes down the costs and its torment to its users.

---

2. Bruce Schneider, *Data and Goliath* (New York: W. W. Norton, 2015), 150.

The cost of producing, exploiting, protecting, and stealing data = the cost of Being-Global.

The system is designed to keep data moving and thus to keep *us* moving, physically and conceptually. Even if I am sitting down, parts of me are moving about. But the best is if I move, or make something move, like a package or money in my bank account:

A full two-thirds of the 24 publicly traded U.S. Internet companies worth more than $1 billion are digital transaction firms. The billion-dollar club includes a heavy dose of travel, local and real estate businesses. The list includes Priceline, Expedia, TripAdvisor, HomeAway, Groupon, OpenTable, Yelp and Zillow. Other transaction-focused businesses that clear the threshold include Amazon, Ebay, Netflix, Vistaprint, Shutterfly, Ancestry, Bankrate and IAC/Match.com. Other than Amazon, very few of these firms deal in physical goods.[3]

1994: "Where do you want to go today?" Microsoft advertising slogan
1997: Priceline
2000: TripAdvisor
2001: Expedia
2005: HomeAway

From FedEx to TedX to EdX to EarthX

The idea of a global world as an abstraction is nonsense. It is a living, breathing entity composed of umpteen billion mobilized, trackable, findable, discoverable, ontological microshards from the size of a planet to the size of microbe. The more we/they travel, the warmer the system becomes. By travel, I do not mean just moving from place to place. Travel via Google Earth, for example, gives Google a huge amount of information. You create a constantly lengthening trail of interaction data, including zoom level, size of map, time and date, location, and your IP address. Even clicking Print or E-mail is an act that is registered and processed by Google's data crunchers.[4]

3. Bruce Upbin, "The Surest Way to Build a Billion-Dollar Internet Company," *Forbes*, March 3, 2013, http://www.forbes.com/sites/bruceupbin/2013/04/03/the-surest-way-to-build-a-billion-dollar-internet-company.

4. Greg Conti, *Googling Security: How Much Does Google Know about You?* (Upper Saddle River, N.J.: Addison-Wesley, 2009), 181.

Sports are the perfect place to naturalize data-enhanced/-ing human activity. Moving bodies: moving balls; organizing fans: organizing data. From metrics to money:

> The leading minds in sports convened in Boston last week at the annual MIT Sloan Sports Analytics Conference (March 2014) to share ideas about how big data will be a game-changer for fans, players, coaches, officials and front-office personnel.[5]

There is no up and down, high and low, but scales of measurable activity and reactivity.

In April 2012, Northern Ireland became the first part of the United Kingdom to require microchipping of individually licensed dogs. England will have mandatory microchipping of all dogs by 2016. Are humans next?

> Yahoo (YHOO +0.25%) has improved employee morale and productivity by providing all of its full- and part-time employees with their choice of an Apple (AAPL−0.86%) iPhone, a Samsung or HTC Android phone, or a Nokia Windows phone. In addition to enabling remote connectivity, faster browsing, and downloading capabilities, the initiative helped Yahoo employees better understand what their customers are using and thus to develop mobile services aligned with market needs.[6]

> No matter what kind of GPS tracking service business you start, you will need to provide your customers with a way to view the movement and position of the assets they are tracking or that you are tracking for them. Rather than trying to develop it alone, choose GPS tracking software that will scale with your business.[7]

5. Lauren Brousell, "8 Ways Big Data and Analytics Will Change Sports," CIO, March 13, 2014, http://www.cio.com/article/2377954/data-management/data-management-8-ways-big-data-and-analytics-will-change-sports.html. See also Tom Brewster, "Hole in One: How Big Data Can Turn Players into Winners," *The Guardian*, September 11, 2014, http://www.theguardian.com/technology/datablog/2014/sep/12/hole-in-one-how-big-data-can-turn-players-into-winners.

6. Ramez Shehadi and Danny Karam, "Five Essential Elements of the Digital Workplace," *Forbes*, March 31, 2014, http://www.forbes.com/sites/boozandcompany/2014/03/31/five-essential-elements-of-the-digital-workplace.

7. "Starting Your Own GPS Tracking Business—How to Begin," Position Logic, May 16, 2013, http://www.positionlogic.com/running-gps-tracking

Old-fashioned, dial-up computer connections, developed in 1989, used to hiss and growl when they were turned on to let you hear them working—to let you know that the connection was being made and tested. "Engineering at work." We came to understand the growl as a connection that was both powerful and fragile at the same time. That was old school, driven by the need to disconnect you from one life and connect you to another—through your carpel tunnels. The engineer wanted the user to feel, acoustically at least, the hard labor that the computer was preparing to do on the human's behalf. It was off or on. The growling computer was the last great hurrah to the modern world of *ergonomics*—from the Greek ργον, meaning "work," and νόμος, meaning "natural law."

The natural law of work died some ten years ago, if not earlier. Today, silence reigns. The Web crawler does the work.

A Being-Global person cannot disconnect. Not even turning the computer off serves to disconnect us. We are bound up in a system that we cannot see but that is everywhere—a force without an apparent workforce:

> In this paper, we experimentally evaluate the qualitative performance of several community detection algorithms using large-scale email networks. The email networks were generated from real email traffic and contain both legitimate email (ham) and unsolicited email (spam). We compare the quality of the algorithms with respect to a number of structural quality functions and a logical quality measure, which assesses the ability of the algorithms to separate ham and spam emails by clustering them into distinct com-munities.[8]

The battery: I have to tend to it, feed it, and protect it. This is my small, ritualistic act of devotion to the great algorithmic deities. But soon, just like the motor, which has more or less disappeared from our consciousness, so too the battery. It is the last vestige from a mechanical age. Already, if the battery dies, it can be resurrected, no Eucharist required.

-business/starting-your-own-gps-tracking-business-how-to-begin.

8. Farnaz Moradi, Tomas Olovsson, and Philippas Tsigas, "An Evaluation of Community Detection Algorithms on Large-Scale Email Traffic," 2012, http://www.syssec-project.eu/m/page-media/3/moradi-sea12.pdf.

> When your phone dies, God knows what can happen.
> —MOPHIES battery phone case ad

Indeed! God knows.

If old-fashioned Being-in-the-World was about bodies that measured speed in trains, cars, and airplanes, Being-Global measures speed by the motion of fingers across the screen.

Two fingers down. Three fingers across. Being-Global measures speed by the motion of eyes. I can now point an infrared beam in my phone and it will tell me if the vegetables in the store are ripe. "Armed with more information, we will soon have a greater understanding of what in this world is good—and what is just rotten."[9] Ha ha. Soon I can point this at you!

A Being-Global person does not recognize a hard line between the real and the extended real. Yes, going into pure fantasy in a game is possible, but the post-ontological world is designed not to be fantasy but to enhance our Self. Taking a hike where your friends can chart your progress, your heartbeat, your sweat, in real time on Google Earth and Instagram is just as real:

> Weaver kept a Germin Foretrex 201 GPS unit with him at all times, to record his latitude, longitude, altitude, and time at 10-second intervals. The 67,000-plus track points collected during the ninety tracking days constitute the Time and Location dimension of the digital footprint.[10]

The post-ontological body no longer fits into the Vitruvian/Leonardo framework of geometry and proportion, no longer conforms to the securities of the mandala or the ritualized *li* of the Confucians. But nor does the body find itself as some hyper-alienated projection of the arbitrary fantasies of power. The post-ontological body is neither fully representable nor fully repressible:

> *Persona* GLOBAL° performance solutions have been culturally adapted and delivered by over 1,400 certified organizational development practitioners and trainers around the world, in as many as

---

9. Mike Ross, "Rotten or Not?," *Boston Globe,* February 2, 2015, A11.

10. Stephen D. Weaver and Mark Gahegan, "Constructing, Visualizing, and Analyzing a Digital Footprint," *Geographical Review* 97, no. 3 (2007): 331.

38 languages. Currently, our performance solutions are deployed in more than 50% of Fortune 1000 companies in 71 countries.[11]

There are no IQ demands for Being-Global. We measure ourselves by our settings. Chess, level 3. Angry Birds, level 22. Dictionary quiz, level 6. Far Cry, level 10 . . . level up!

We once thought that bodies consisted of organs with functions. We now know that our bodies are really just vast microbial universes that, in the accumulation of molecular and cellular specializations and activities, produce the effect that we know as consciousness-of-life. Post-ontology builds on this awareness. The vast accumulation of invisible algorithms and codes cumulatively produces the effect that we know as consciousness-of-life.

Microbes + Algorithms = Life.

Being-Global is to live in an *infested,* bio-onto-mathematical environment—to live *freely*—"freely"—freely?

The Global Personality Inventory—Adaptive (GPI-A) . . . uses Computer Adaptive Testing (CAT) technology, which means the assessment automatically adjusts to personality traits by asking questions based on previous responses. This results in a unique, brief, and secure testing experience. The GPI-A is intended for use in the selection and development of employees.[12]

Being-Global does not come cheap. It needs massive amounts of electricity, along with batteries, nickel, rubber, Teflon, titanium, microchips—a vast supply chain of production. Data centers—like the multi-billion-dollar Google data center on the Columbia River in Oregon—consume up to 1.5 percent of all the electricity in the world.

Internet freedom is the skin ointment that makes the contaminated/contaminating body feel good.

The dark side of Being-Global is environmental degradation on a vast scale. Our complicity is complete. Being-Global does not ask technical questions about mineral extraction. Nor do the great de-

11. See Persona Global, http://www.personaglobal.com/.

12. See CEB SHL Talent Management, http://ceb.shl.com/uk/solutions/products/docs/fact_sheet-global%20personality%20inventory_adaptive_UKE.pdf.

ities want you to know! All we know is that they/we live in clouds as if the earth minerals that make all this happen do not even exist!

> Not all clouds are created equal. Here is why the new SOS is the best offer on Earth.[13]

> SavvyMart employs RFID sensors and smart shopping carts to track what its customers are putting in their shopping carts in near real-time. They are also tracking where their customers are going and the patterns they follow through stores. Rather than wait to store and mine this data, they have designed a predictive model that spots trends in products purchased together. . . . Managers use a product placement data mash-up application to suggest end-stand arrangements that optimize related product purchase opportunities based on the evolution of cart patterns and product purchases.[14]

13. See SOS Online Backup, http://www.sosonlinebackup.com/.

14. Brian Hopkins, "The Anthropology of Data," CIO, October 20, 2010, http://www.cio.com/article/2372429/enterprise-architecture/the-anthropology-of-data.html.

4. Onto-Modeling

We always come back to the human equation.

—DATA in "Code of Honor," *Star Trek: The Next Generation* (1987)

JUST AS WE ARE PART of complex social formations that leave lasting impressions on our sense of identity, we also give off ontological elements—*onto-bits*—into the digital ecosystem. In some instances, these onto-bits are designed to seem to enhance our sense-of-Self. They can even be used to ostensibly protect us, but they are also used against us to irritate Being, to humiliate it, observe it, overtly and covertly:

> We are data people, we believe in the prospect of uncovering "invisible" data to help make sense of all of the consuming, driving, walking, running, watching, eating and buying that is going on in the "real-world" [via infomatics].[1]

Our onto-bits coalesce into something blandly called Data, but this Data is *only* useful in the form of surplus, and data surplus *only* works when it exceeds the capacity of data processing. Data is a compulsive self-propagator. All data equals more data.

THE SECOND LAW OF POST-ONTOLOGICAL THERMODYNAMICS
"Data" = Data Surplus > Data Processing.

The incongruity of surplus and process is not a design flaw but a design requirement to produce the necessary friction that holds

---

1. Location Genius, http://www.viainformatics.com/.

the post-ontological together. The more, the better, meaning that data as a system of comprehension is just one small step back from its own incomprehensibility.

Capitalism = Data Deficit Anxiety Syndrome.

This syndrome produces a continual spinning of the wheels, wherein just enough surplus is produced to not quite overwhelm the system. However, the calculations must always appear to be overwhelming the system as a way to push the drive toward the renaturalization of the Self.

Data Mining, Data Enrichment, Data Aggregation, Data Processing, Data Preprocessing, Data Extraction, Data Harmonization, Data Masking, Data Consolidation, Data Mapping. In the process, we are continuously being (data) trimmed, (data) smoothed, (Kalman) filtered, and Winsorized!

> **1986**: Principles of Data Mining and Knowledge Discovery (First European Conference)
>
> **1988**: Barry Devlin and Paul Murphy, "An Architecture for a Business and Information System." The term business data warehouse is introduced.[2]
>
> **2000**: One of the earliest uses of the term *Big Data* was by F. X. Diebold in "Big Data Dynamic Factor Models for Macroeconomic Measurement and Forecasting."[3]

The following quotation from a specialist on the topic of data mining reflects an assumption of optimism as well as the transparent confidence that the question of *uncertainty* will help data miners better "manipulate uncertain events." We understand both the truth and falsity of the claim:

2. B. A. Devlin and P. T. Murphy, "An Architecture for a Business and Information System," *IBM Systems Journal* 27 (1988), http://www.ieeexplore.ieee.org/.

3. As presented at the Eighth World Congress of the Econometric Society in Seattle, August 2000. Subsequently published in M. Dewatripont, L. P. Hansen, and S. Turnovsky, eds., *Advances in Economics and Econometrics: Eighth World Congress of the Econometric Society*, 115–22 (Cambridge: Cambridge University Press, 2003).

Modeling uncertainty is a necessary component of almost all data analysis. Indeed, in some cases our primary aim is to model the uncertain or random aspects of data. It is one of the great achievements of science that we have developed a deep and powerful understanding of uncertainty. The capricious gods that were previously invoked to explain the lack of predictability in the world have been replaced by mathematical, statistical, and computer-based models that allow us to understand and manipulate uncertain events. We can even attempt the seemingly impossible and predict uncertain events, where prediction for a data miner either can mean the prediction of future events (where the notion of uncertainty is very familiar) or prediction in a non-temporal sense of a variable whose true value is somehow hidden from us (for example, diagnosing whether a person has cancer, based on only descriptive symptoms).[4]

Such technorealism has nothing to do with post-ontology. We need to avoid telling the story of the human through the notion of first principles just as much as through the story of technological advancement. The real point is that the uncertainty of data is a fact of life, a fact of being Human—designed into our flesh and bones.

If we can envision the modern world as a world of the X-ray that erases the surface of the body and that renders into the visual realm a hard and a soft, a Being-Global lives in a world of ir/radiation. We have replaced inner organs with proximity organs—mostly made of titanium, glass, chips, and rubber—some visible, others invisible, all designed. We can attach these organs physically, or nearby, or even halfway across the world. The purpose of these "devices" is to produce, magnify, and expose our ontic exhaust. But already they are not enough to do the necessary work. Engineers are now finding ways to turn our eyes, skin, and corporeal evaporations into data providers.

Data mountains, data streams, data leakages, data fogs, data peaks, data collapses, data storms, data deluges, data explosions, digital pollution, and data havens. To move through this landscape, businesses now need something called Data Dogs that sniff out opportunities and lap them up with Data Tongues. It all gets placed in Data Warehouses and Data Marts.

We are an algorithmic heuristic.

4. David Hand, Heikki Mannila, and Padhraic Smyth, *Principles of Data Mining* (Cambridge, Mass.: The MIT Press, 2001).

Computation—if one can even use that antiquated word—involves at its core an analytic secrecy for which no external or internal analysis can account. Computation only works if there is *more* computation. It is a science (to use another strange-sounding word) that revolves around the calculation of instability—the calculation of a calculated instability—leading to the incalculable (but predictably unpredictable) calculation of instability. My "I" is irrevocably dependent on and complicit in these productive and *counter*productive layers of algorithmic activities.

In the world of data excess, algorithms chop us into digestible/ marketable/governable/hackable categories. The police have a different model of me than my health provider, my bank, Google, or the IRS. Because "I" can never really see my own "I," I am forced to rely on these metrics as indicators of my social presence. The algorithm represents us, *not* as complete beings, but as slices through/across our Beings.

These algorithmic slices operate on the individual to fulfill a sublimated desire for completion. They are created in our image, and thus the more, the better, as they, in their emerging cumulativeness, fulfill a range of needs from the narcissistic to the epistemological, from the masochistic to the liberational, and from the seductive to the performative:

> In the Quantified Self community we focus on projects and ideas that help people access and get meaning out their personal data, including the information you can collect with your smartphone. If you have an iPhone, Android, or Windows phone you're already carrying one of the world's most sophisticated self-tracking tools. The GPS, accelerometer, the microphone, all of these tiny sensors make up a great set of tools you can use to understand how you move around the world.[5]

> Third-party data providers are everywhere. How do you get the information you truly need without investing aimlessly?[6]

---

5. Ernesto Ramirez, "How to Map Your Moves Data," Quantified Self, March 14, 2014, http://quantifiedself.com/2014/03/map-moves-data.

6. Andrew Frank, "The Perfect Match: Finding Your Ideal Data Provider," Gartner for Marketing Leaders, https://www.gartner.com/marketing/digital/research/data-driven/find-a-data-provider.

Wiland Services—which recognizes the Oracle of Oracles!—maintains a digital database of thousands of points of information on almost 300 million individuals and more than 110 million households. It collects this information for clients to help them better predict and manage their target populations. According to Wiland's website,

> the Wiland database [doesn't] just process and store the data. The data is mapped very strategically to create maximum predictive marketing response power across thousands of variables. The database is also unique in another very important respect: it is a truly exclusive, private resource for participating clients only. . . . That's our 1, 2, 3 advantage: the best data; the best analytics; focus on quality, so client marketing dollars go further and produce more. In short, we deliver a better future for our clients—a future of better results for their marketing dollar.[7]

> The DataBlast client enables the user to interact with the data warehouse through a series of modules, each specifically tailored to deliver intuitive yet powerful functionality.[8]

These warehouses are not really warehouses with data just sitting there passively on shelves. These warehouses are actually biological machines performing a wide range of activities, whether useful or not: data normalization, data sanitation, data profiling, data reconciliation, data sovereignty, data dashboarding. Data binding. Data buffering. They eat more data and even suffer occasionally from Data Cholesterol.

To naturalize all of this, to make it *seem* that it is working for us, to enmesh us in its disinhibiting project, data companies pretend to give us access to some of the information. ChoicePoint and LexisNexis, for example, have compiled vast amounts of personal data that they routinely sell to interested parties. For a fee, of course, individuals can gain access to personal data: records relating to adoption, birth, police, ancestry, divorce, death, FBI, and so on.

WineStein is a software algorithm used in European and U.S. restaurants and shopping markets. WineStein calculates the

7. "Direct Mail," Wiland Solutions, http://www.wiland.com/channel /direct-mail.

8. Datablast, http://www.datablast.com/.

taste and aromatic aspects of the dish you are preparing and gives you a suitable wine recommendation:

> Basically, we convert everything that matters in a wine & food match into numbers. How exactly is the chef's secret, of course, and like good cooks, we'll never tell. However, we can tell you that once WineStein has done the "basic" math on what you tell it you want to eat, it will start a search among the over 50,000 examples of wine & food pairings (and mispairings!) that it was "trained" with.[9]

If the term *capitalism* belonged to the nineteenth and twentieth centuries, the new term is *data capitalism*. All capitalism is data capitalism.

The issue is not how data capitalism is going to change social structures, improve health (as it often claims), make governments more secure (i.e., less secure), and improve the flow of commerce (i.e., make some people fabulously wealthy). These can all be promoted and debated, as can how many billions in revenue Big Data generates (about $62 billion in the United States in 2012).[10] Today, the information sector is probably about 6 percent of the U.S. gross domestic product (GDP).

It is all too easy to see data capitalism as an expanded form of imperialism, with nothing better to do than to exploit, consume, and destroy, and to later moralize about freedom and wealth. Data Capitalism is beset by an inner torment unknown to early capitalist ages. The algorithms that it creates have their own libidinal needs and have infested the host. They have become irrevocably embedded in capitalism's (dis)functionality.

The human is a data derivative, packaged, formatted, and protected for the global stock market of information.

The irony is that whereas the subject (the "I") remains relatively stabile in its ability to self-affirm (the lingering *by-product* of the psychologizing of the modern Self), objectivity (as in the social sciences) collapses into the illusions produced by the global cyclone of the infomatic industry:

9. WineStein, http:/www.winestein.com/.

10. Elizabeth Dwoskin, "Study: Digital Marketing Industry Worth $62 Billion," *Wall Street Journal,* October 14, 2013, http://blogs.wsj.com /digits/2013/10/14/study-digital-marketing-industry-worth-62-billion.

DNA as storage: a team of scientists from the European Bioinformatics Institute reportedly stored a complete set of Shakespeare's sonnets, a PDF of the first paper to describe DNA's double helix structure, a 26-second mp3 clip from Martin Luther King Jr.'s "I Have a Dream" speech, a text file of a compression algorithm, and a JPEG photograph in a strand of DNA.[11]

Corporations keep enemies at bay by fictionalizing their holdings. It is called Data Masking and Data Fictionalization.[12] Such fictionalization is, of course, reversible with the proper code. The body may look different, in the eyes of potential violators, but the bones are not changed. So the fact remains that each data point is a fact. Even if it is scrubbed, cleaned, processed, and fictionalized, it is still somewhere an empirical entity, but just as it is not passive, it is not data unless it is protected, locked away behind layers of firewalls. The entire system of humanity is microprocessed through the grid of sequestered empiricism. It is a system that knows seduction but no joy. In the end, as humans become more encrypted, even their joy will become just another manufactured product.

Data is now our ontological vitamin.

Data is the extended space of ontological occupation—of de-ontological deoccupation.

From ontology to dataology (the study of data) and back, but back to what?

Human = Δ = $\Delta1$ = $\Delta2$ = $\Delta3$, etc. (where Δ means "change")

"Data in the raw" is littered with useless noise, irrelevant information, and misleading patterns. To convert this into that precious thing we are after requires a study of its properties and the discovery of a working model that captures the behavior we are interested in. Being in posses-

11. Desire Athow, "World Could Run Out of Storage Capacity within Two Years Warns Seagate," Tech Radar Pro, December 22, 2014, http://www.techradar.com/us/news/internet/data-centre/world-could-run-out-of-storage-capacity-within-2-years-warns-seagate-vp-1278040/2.

12. "Fictionalization," Gladstone, http://www.gladstonecomputer.com/?page_id=309. See also *Database Real Application Testing User's Guide,* Oracle Database, https://docs.oracle.com/cd/E11882_01/server.112/e41481/tdm_data_masking.htm#RATUG4011.

sion of a model despite the noise means an organization now owns the beginnings of further discovery and innovation.[13]

Data comes from Activity. Data is a record of what happens. But if you are not party to the activity when it happens, your chance of capturing data is lost—forever.[14]

Data capital flywheel creates a competitive advantage that is *very* hard to catch . . . no company is left untouched.[15]

There were five exabytes of information at the dawn of civilization through 2003, but that much information is now created every two days, and the pace is increasing.[16]

Society is nothing but an onto-laboratory. Thousands of people are gainfully employed designing ways to study us and our most intimate activities and habits—the world over, waiting for, or silently producing/anticipating/lusting for, more information. It is a ghost anthropology:

Internet Presence Management (IPM) . . . is the process of controlling or influencing the Web presence, or Internet-based channels, of an or-

13. "In the world of data this expertise in converting is called Data Science. The reason it takes a science to convert a raw resource into something of value is because what is extracted from the 'ground' is never in a useful form. 'Data in the raw' is littered with useless noise, irrelevant information, and misleading patterns. To convert this into that precious thing we are after requires a study of its properties and the discovery of a working model that captures the behavior we are interested in. Being in possession of a model despite the noise means an organization now owns the beginnings of further discovery and innovation. Something unique to their business that has given them the knowledge of what to look for, and the codified descriptions of a world that can now be mechanized and scaled." Sean McClure, "Data Science and Big Data: Two very Different Beasts," KDnuggets, July 6, 2015, http://www.kdnuggets.com/2015/07/data-science-big-data-different-beasts.html.

14. Margaret Harrist, "What's Next for Big Data," Oracle, http://www.oracle.com/us/corporate/features/big-data-predictions/index.html.

15. Ibid.

16. Eric Schmidt, former CEO of Google, quoted in Liran Einav and Jonathan Levin, "The Data Revolution and Economic Analysis," National Bureau of Economic Research, 2014, http://web.stanford.edu/~jdlevin/Papers/BigData.pdf.

ganization or company, with the goal of increasing that entity's online presence and overall Internet efficiency.[17]

And yet, who we are cannot be traced from the human side of the equation, much less from the analytic side. "I" am untraceable. An ethnographer can interview me and move into my house and become part of my family and community, but, even after years, she would have no better understanding of "me" than I would. There is no ethnography that can explain my existence. The algorithmic pulses of the banks know more about me than any ethnographer.

We are now told that our onto-bits have feelings too. The humanization of data is the last phase of our post-ontological development. Do we want to save lives in Africa, or do we want to save unused data?

> Each month, millions of unused data are taken back by wireless companies. Tragic. . . . Please. Help save the data!
> —T-MOBILE ADVERTISEMENT featuring Kim Kardashian

> Hey Father . . . you've got unlimited data from Boost Mobile. Do it! He will never know. Thaaaat's it Father, Come to Data [the Devil].
> —BOOST MOBILE ADVERTISEMENT, 2015

> A better network doesn't mess with your data.
> —VERIZON ADVERTISEMENT, 2015

What would an anthropology of our unused data look like?

How much of "me" is me? I dare any ontologist to answer that question.

Anthropology, as it developed in the nineteenth and twentieth centuries, assumed the primacy of the human body, on one hand, and the naturalness of sociopolitical relations, on the other hand. But this now-classic sense of the individual and of its associated abstractions of labor, power, and religion, as forces that objectify the subject, is inadequate to the theoretical task at hand, which is to get a grasp on an animated ontology in which subject position and object position are indistinguishable. Conventional ideas of theory, method, and philosophy are becoming inoperable. The

---

17. Webopedia, s.v. "presence," http://www.webopedia.com/TERM/P /presence.html.

only field left is that of a *practical* ontology that allows me a range of options from feeling totally enclosed to feeling totally empowered; from being obsessively interested to totally disinterested; from being a malicious predator to a self-righteous protector. Post-ontology forces these extremes to the surface for it to justify its existence.

It is, therefore, not possible to organize these extremes into the standard observational matrixes of anthropology, because victimization, for example, does not match with victimhood, unless one wants to make sweeping and useless generalizations that lead one either to celebrate the digital and its self-projected ecology of potential or to retreat into a shell of despair and complaint, both of which are often paraded as theory or, worse yet, as philosophy.

What we need is an anthroalgorithmology. Anything less would continue to place the primacy of the body, and its will-oriented, social connections, at the center of the conversation. Anthroalgorithmology acknowledges that the human and its (dis-/re-)embodied computational signifiers are on equal footing. Algorithms complete us, and we complete them, but never fully, and on purpose, so as to always create an anthrocentric illusion. There is always an algorithm that can overcome the previous one, just as there are humans who can and are in fact designed to surprise the algorithm-producing deities by their unexpected actions. Thus the continual struggle by the deities to "innovate"; the continual struggle to "protect" and "promote"; the continual effort to contractualize the human into submission and servitude.

The age of anthrocentrism is over.

5. Onto-Graphies

IN THE OLD DAYS, we talked about fishing, farming, mining, and writing; now it is Phishing, Pharming, Mining, and Scripting.

Feeling overweight? No, I do not mean you; I mean your software!

"Software Bloat: How to Get in Shape"
"How to Deal with Bloatware"[1]

I am not speaking here of the language of mathematics that is known only to the high priests and their functionaries. I am speaking of a language that operates through the host language, displaced and displacing, appearing and disappearing. It entangles itself in the host language to familiarize/defamiliarze a world of otherwise unknowable and mysterious operations. Its strongest attachment is, of course, to English. Yet, even in other languages, its traces are increasingly apparent.

We employ this language in different ways: (1) as an attribute of our modernity ("Please Google ontology"); (2) as a way to communicate with the digital deities, their intermediaries, and the IT specialists ("Where are my output parameters in Grasshopper?"); (3) *on* us to clarify/obfuscate our positionality/depositionality in the world ("Contact us"; click; "Oops, this page no longer exists").

But there is something else happening, a new cognition—one as slippery as the human itself. We live and breathe in a vast new world of metaphors, double entendres, puns, euphemisms, allusions, neologisms, homonyms, and satiric misspellings. The post-ontological is a zone of rhetorical epistemologies and epis-

1. Hiawatha Bray, "Software Bloat? How to Get in Shape," *Boston Globe*, March 5, 2015, C1.

temological rhetoric. We *are* the rhetorical effect. We are Meta-onto-phors.

In the old days, people collected apples in bushels. Now we connect Apples by means of Bushels.

A Being-Global person enters into loops of language not via the process of thought but through a vast array of code words that define our everyday practices, life-worlds, life-objects, live-links . . .

People/Peeple. The words have different meanings in that one re-fers to humans, the other to an app, but technically, *peeple* is not a ho-mophone (which are words that sound alike but have different mean-ings). The name of the app plays on the name of humans. Furthermore, because *peeple* is a neologism, its status as word is not yet secure.

Such quirks of language, formerly known only to those with a PhD in English literature, are now the new norm: mondegreens, spooner-isms, portmanteaus, and malapropisms abound, and are trademarked.

The word *link* comes from Old Danish *lænkia*, or "chain," as in "chain mail," the protective vest that warriors wore. Links are the pro-tection of our new post-ontology, covering and defining our thoughts and communications. Like all armor, they are vulnerable to attack—to viruses, bugs, trojans, heisenbugs, bots—that enter and damage the invisible soft tissue. Being-Global knows that the links are themselves not free. They are controlled, manipulated, constructed—a Candyland of possibilities, a minefield of deceptions.

"Data friendly" means encrypted against the NSA.

Cookies, Flash cookies, zombie cookies. Without them, we are nothing, along with ham, spam, bacon, spaghetti—the new (in)diges-tional consciousness:[2]

BACON: Blocked Adaptive Computationally efficient outlier Nominators[3]

Spam and ham processors specify special actions to take when you exit a group buffer. Spam processors act on spam messages, and ham proces-sors on ham messages.[4]

---

2. A. K. Dewdney, "On the Spaghetti Computer and Other Analog Gadgets for Problem Solving," *Scientific American,* June 1984, 19–26.

3. Nedret Billor, Ali S. Hadi, and Paul F. Velleman, "BACON: Blocked Adaptive Computationally Efficient Outlier Nominators," *Computational Statistics and Data Analysis* 34, no. 3 (2000): 279–329, http://www.sciencedirect.com/science/article/pii/S0167947399001012.

4. "Spam and Ham Processors," GNU Operating System, http://

Not horizon, but Verizon. Not mobile, but T-Mobile. Not fast, but Sprint. Not map, but Habitation Station. The territory of Being-Global is not a solid color with boundaries, as nations are colored on maps. There are gaps, coverage holes, empty areas, where connections are dropped—a word so common now that one hardly hears the humor. These areas are known as "dead zones."

Our auditory language has changed too. The Being-Global lives with notifications, vibrations, buzzes, alerts, chimes, silent modes, and airplane modes. Plug-ins. Flash. Controllers are not people, but things. Do we control them? Do they control us? What do they control, actually?

Replace the word "water" with "data" in this ad for an Android app:

> Do you drink enough water? Do you always forget to drink water regularly? This App reminds you to drink water every day and tracks your water drinking habits.
>
> You only need to enter your current weight and Drinking Water will help you to determine how much water your body needs everyday. When you have finished drinking a cup of water, you will need to add a cup in the app.
>
> Benefits of drinking water:
>
> • You stay in shape, as it's calorie free
>
> • You can clear up your skin
>
> • You keep your skin and nails healthy
>
> • Your fitness will increase

If our post-ontological Being is hydrated by data, it is animated by a degravitationalized semiotic at the distant periphery of which are the programmers and IT people. There is a whole sublanguage to describe them: hackers, hacktivists, white hats, black hats, skiddies, Certified Ethical Hackers. . . . They are all part of the great Higgs field of Being. (A Higgs field is a field that, unlike the more familiar electromagnetic field, cannot be turned off but instead takes a nonzero constant value almost everywhere.)

Being-Global lives in a post-poetic world: a poetry that we hardly hear, though it surrounds us. A flood of text messages,

---

www.gnu.org/software/emacs/manual/html_node/gnus/Spam-and-Ham-Processors.html.

SMSs, and multimedia message displays. Not words but pass-words. Not texts but scripts. IDC ("I don't care").

Silicon, Aztec, Oracle, Sapphire, Symantec, Amplify, Access, Invite. Morph, Mommy Save. Administrator. Bake. Cockroach. Crog. Word.

I have a Galaxy in my pocket!

The word *privacy,* like the word *security,* is just another in the long list of poetic euphemisms. The Convention for the Protection of Individuals with Regard to Automatic Processing of Personal Data, passed by the European Union in 1981, extends the safeguards for people's rights and fundamental freedoms, in particular "the right to the respect for privacy." But what does that mean: "the right to the *respect* for privacy"? Obviously, just the opposite!

The word *privacy* means soon-to-not-be-private. Not even Hillary Clinton understood this most basic rule of post-ontology. Privacy is just a box I click on the screen. It is one among millions of algorithms designed to render privacy moot.

The word *privacy,* like so many of our words, is a survival from our ontological antiquity. The same is true for the entire range of philosophy-inducing terms: *body, soul, spirit, community.* We may continue to speak them out of a type of laziness, but in truth we have no way to define them.

The data-enhancing deities remove semiotic clarity in order—ironically enough—to clarify the location of the human while at the same time enhancing misunderstanding as the very oil in the machine.

The newly coded, encoded, supracoded, encrypted world speaks, of course, to the impossibility of ever understanding the code itself. Turning and twisting, the semiotic sphere of Being defines a space of enjoyment and parody, of projections and protections, creating a textual unconscious for which there is no object apart from the dis-placed relationship between human and reason. After feeding on language's mimetic function, this new language slides past any ob-ligation to the signified. Etymological historicism is at an end. The era of the paternalistic emphasis on *logos* is no more. The age of the dictionary is over.

The lingoification, poetification, rhetoricifcation, punification of language is more than just the casual or joyful dissonance of slang. Nor should this linguistic inventiveness be seen as simply a coating of sugar over exploitative processes. It is the expression of an unerring instinct that deflects our gaze from the tasks at hand, protecting ac-tors, creators, and perpetrators alike. It serves as a lure, on one hand,

and, on the other hand, as a veiled warning. We speak it with a wink and a nod while the code makers quietly do their job, speaking/writing their more esoteric codes.

The pleasure of (dis)association points to the complete failure of conventional language to address the future, when the code will finally reveal itself for all to see. But the magic of our new metaphoric and euphemistic discourse is that the Promised Land can only recede from view as the language that evokes it becomes denser and drifts in and out of use and memory.

Speaking this language is not a speaking out of the schizophrenic Otherness of the electronic world, if by "schizophrenia" we mean a helpless collapse into voices from another world. On the contrary, it is the natural extension of ontological energy. It is the glue that binds everything together. It is not the ornament to language; it is not some affectation prompted by marketing strategies but the very structure on which our new, extended consciousness is built. It is a challenge to language itself, stitching into the already-made a loop of excitement that flashes before us the originary sense of discovery, opportunity, and promise, even if those loops in their global proliferations enclose the Human, with a fistlike grip, in a spectral operation.

This linguistic–semantic space lies at the overlap of Being and Global. It is *the* point of contact between the two, between the ontological and the deontological. It is slippery zone where mortals and deities can speak to each other as the subject of a subject. The subject of an absent subject. The possible subject-to-be of a possible subject-that-was-and-will-possibly-be.

If we burrow down to the actual written efforts of our new managers, we are certain to be impressed even there. From data to Dada. The syntax of a KQML message can look, brilliantly, like this:

```
(ask-one
:sender jane
:content (stack_paint ?stack)
:receiver paint-server :ontology PSL)
```

where ask-one is a KQML performative, and sender, content, receiver, and ontology are its arguments. In this example, stack_paint is an intermediate queue, i.e., a resource-related concept that can be expressed using PSL terminology.[5]

5. Line Pouchard, Nenad Ivezic, and Craig Schlenoff, "Ontology

Even punctuation marks have new and exciting roles:

```
proc abs max = ([,]real a, ref real y, ref int i, k)real:[6]
```

We now only find desire within the zone of semiotic incomprehension:

```
comment The absolute greatest element of the matrix a, of size ⌊a by 2⌊a
is transferred to y, and the subscripts of this element to i and k; comment
begin
    real y := 0; i := ⌊a; k := 2⌊a;
    for p from ⌊a to ⌊a do
        for q from 2⌊a to 2⌊a do
            if abs a[p, q] > y then
                y := abs a[p, q];
                i := p; k := q
            fi
        od
    od;
y
end # abs max #[7]
```

Engineering for Distributed Collaboration in Manufacturing," paper presented at the AIS 2000 Conference, March 2000.

    6. Wikipedia, s.v. "ALGOL," https://en.wikipedia.org/wiki/ALGOL.

    7. Ibid.

6. Onto-Activations

AGRICULTURAL CIVILIZATIONS OF OLD placed extreme value on sedentarism, largely because they needed people to be predictable. Predictability facilitated governance, taxes, and enforcement. Disruptions were called disasters or the will of the gods. Though the Industrial Age mobilized people in new ways, it too was built around an ideology of enforceable stability, with the factory, city, and plantation becoming the new social and economic units of control. Governments learned to use a mixture of incentives, ideologies, self-indoctrinations, and policing. In all cases, humans were supposed to accommodate themselves to some combination of tradition, belief, texts, law, and force. The Enlightenment philosophers tried to put reason into the mix, but it became just another way to acclimatize people to the necessity of being controlled, some would say for better, some would say for worse. Hegel liked the security of the nation-state; Marx looked forward to his moneyless communes; Heidegger looked backward to small farms. But whether one began with an outer world (ritual or nation) or an inner world (religion or existentialism), one was expected either to conform to a certain viewpoint or then to change oneself *and* thus society in some fashion or another according to preconditioned, procedural principles (conversion, green card application, patriotism, military draft, reason, psychoanalysis, etc.). All of this made Self and Other predictable, identifiable, and exploitable. It is the prime directive of modernity.

The post-ontological world pulls away from the immediacy of such impulses. But it is not anarchic as such. Nation-states with strong centralized governments aim to work against the potential liberatory principle. But a nation-state can only force so much ontic exhaust out of the human if its purpose is primarily restrictive. In such conditions, the algorithmic world is merely an extension of the standard conventions and abuses of power. Democracies, tied in to the perspectives of globalized corporations, prefer a more human world, one with choices that trap the human in the fold of her humanness; that is what generates heat in the system. The great data-consuming deities celebrate the human-being-human as it opens up ever new profit horizons. Algorithms feed on our mistakes and stupidity.

The meaning of the Human has been changed.

We are *not* the consumers of data but the *providers* of data, and our so-called providers are the *consumers.* We have been redomesticated in that respect.

Let me explain.

Romantic philosophy—and much modernist philosophy as well—contrasts embodied experience with an outwardly placed world. That does not go away in the post-ontological; it becomes a necessary illusion. The ontology of experience, instead of being a positive opening to expression, is increasingly a protective shell designed to pretend to isolate Being from its degravitational positioning. Experience becomes a refuge, enhanced, multiplied, and inauthentic (in the traditional sense) but, ironically, all the more authentic as a home-for-being. It lends itself open to exploitation as well as to resistance, though in a sense all resistance is futile. Its first victim is the distinction between the Human and the Inhuman. The duality would normally be identified, depending on where one stands, with concepts like reason versus superstition, feeling versus science, good versus evil, believer versus infidel, and a host of possible perversions and inversions. Old dichotomies have been rendered obsolete. We must now talk of just one thing: (in)human.

That does not mean that the human is now simulacrumized (Jean Baudrillard), only that the human is being pushed into *more* humanness, pushed to its corporeal / sensate / moral / physical / psychological / political / social / environmental / sexual / bacteriological / global limits. We are being reengineered in various invisible dimensions and at various speeds, from the millisecond to the bureaucratic scale of years.

The world of data is not the world of information; it is the world of different temporalities grinding noiselessly against each other.

It is this that I call the (in)human.

The data-consuming deities are invested to the hilt in the immanence of the new (in)human, a water-and-carbon-base surface that emits the life pulse of data. I am more valuable alive than dead, thus the push by the pharmas to keep me alive as long as possible, to give me an erection that will last four hours or a stomach that can be purged of its discomforting gases. They want the human to see bodies in terms of yeast infections, toenail fungus, skin rashes, inflammatory bowel diseases for which the medicine produces an expanding list of secondary symptoms and illnesses. We are a corporeal miasma, pulsating with antibiotics and probiotics that keep the data coming. What tuberculosis was to the nineteenth century, cancer to the twentieth, idiopathic diseases are to the twenty-first (idiopathic disease is defined as a disease that develops without any apparent or known causes):

Virology + cryptovirology = ontovirology.As constructed by quasi-deified entities, the (in)human is both permeable and impermeable, documented and yet never fully documented. It is intended to be enhanced, subverted, and replaced. But even if the supremacy of the Self, as felt in the everyday world, is continually being decentered/recentered, the primacy of our subjectivity as a fantasy of our archaic selves remains as if untouched.

> The U.S. Department of Homeland Security (DHS) has awarded Northrop Grumman Corporation (NYSE:NOC) a contract to begin field-testing a new generation of autonomous biodetection instruments as part of the BioWatch Gen-3 program. Northrop Grumman was awarded the $8.4 million task order under the BioWatch Gen-3 System Performance Demonstration Contract. The total potential value of the contract is $37 million over three years.[1]

Though there is no center to our ontic exhaust—as it is designed in fact to be multicentric—and though it remains blind to what happens inside the Self, its core *dis*functionality opens up a void in which the human becomes (in)human.

Humans can naturalize their (in)humanity in the very name of humanity; it is the Human's greatest skill.

How did this (in)human come about?

---

1. Alleace Gibbs, "Northrop Grumman Begins Testing of DHS BioWatch Gen-3 Biological Detection Program," GlobeNewswire via COMTEX, November 18, 2010, http://investor.northropgrumman.com/phoenix.zhtml ?c=112386&p=irol-newsArticle&ID=1498184&highlight.

From about 3000 BCE onward, we have become slaves to the creation of food surpluses, producing mythologies and an endless set of rituals and ideologies that celebrate the equation between civilization and agriculture. Somewhat similarly, we are now slaves to the creation of data surpluses and have produced a narrative that masterminds and celebrates the liberation of the (in)human imagination. But if the old agricultural–civilizational world was built around predictability, the predictability of seasons, of the moon and sun, of life and death, the new data–civilizational world is built around structural unpredictability. Just in time for global warming: ecology custom made for the data deities.

And like the early agriculturalists of old who fabricated various justifications for their efforts to make the gods *seem* alive (like having to feed the ever-hungry deities in the form of offerings and sacrifices in a worldview that we call "religion"), we have to justify our new relationships as something other than "work." It is no accident that media and entertainment lead the way! To be good "providers," (in)humans have to not simply enjoy themselves but live a *vita activa*; there can be no space for *vita contemplative*—even yoga is now an app.

In the meantime, we are continually growing, harvesting, and exhausting data, even if we do not know it, mostly to give it away to the deities, some of whom will then bill us for its use. But what farmer is forced to give away his crop and is then billed for the use of a tractor?

Interface is the old word. Today it might be known to those in the know as RTSTREAM, which stands for real-time query processing for data streams. The ontology of old has to be replaced by onto-RTSTREAMology.

Companies and governments hoard their data in data granaries, which need to be protected at great expense. But data is not just food for the deities; data is their opium. *They* are addicted to data. *They* cannot live without it. *They* need more and more. (In)humans are the opium providers!

We are all embedded in an agricultural–hallucinogenic environment where we, the (in)humans, provide the drugs (our onto-data) that sustain the healthy relationship with the deities.

A new agricultural worldview is coming into view!

The best way to produce the necessary drug is not just to make (in)human = data but to reduce/magnify the (in)human into an action figure—not in the pop cultural sense but in the sense that everything the (in)human does must be registered through action. If there is no Δ (Δ = change), there is no (in)human:

(in)human = Δ.

The algorithmic–agricultural totality aims not just at the empirical (in)human but at the new, *naturalized* (in)human, an (in)human who does not notice any more its identification with its supraterritorial permeations. The endless task of elastic, approximate modeling, adjusting for the (in)human, constitutes humanity in all its newly productive glory. Like the Heisenberg principle, the closer the deities seem to get to modeling our activities, the more elusive and vulnerable those activities become—are designed to become—even if, in some cases, the end game exposes the actual inhuman of the (in)human:

Human = $\Delta = \Delta^1 = \Delta^2 = \Delta^3 = \Delta^n$ = Data.

A recent headline from NASA Science News states, "Humans Can Become Confused and Disoriented—and Even a Little Queasy—in an Alien World Where Up and Down Have No Meaning." You wonder, *Which way is up? And where are my arms and legs?* Throw in a dash of vertigo and occasional mild illusions and you're beginning to sense what it can be like to live "in orbit."[2] It seems to me that this actually describes the situation here on earth.

Back in the sixteenth century, calculus placed the sun firmly at the center of the universe. The "Copernican Revolution," as Immanuel Kant phrased it in his *Critique of Pure Reason* (1787), was even used as a metaphor to explain the effect of reason in Enlightenment thinking. But whether this was good or bad (Karl Marx equated calculus with capitalism) is now irrelevant. The new calculus embodies a resistance to the primacy of the Euclidean world, which begins with zero and moves in upward and downward motions to infinity and back. Because it is binary, the new mathematics has no real zero. Zero is simply a Not-One. A One is a Not-Zero. The open-ended nature of binary thinking destabilizes both the classical and modern notions of science.

2. "Mixed Up in Space," *NASA Science News*, August 7, 2001, http://science.nasa.gov/science-news/science-at-nasa/2001/ast07aug_1.

7. Onto-Social

BEFORE BUDDHA INVENTED RENUNCIATION; before Christians invented martyrdom; before Mohammed invented the jihad, before the Hebrews invented monotheism, before Plato invented the dreaded cave in which we supposedly live, blind to the presence of all that is Good, people talked to each other in freer ways. They talked to dead ancestors, to rocks, to trees, to animals, to spirits. A Being-Global world returns us to ancient possibilities, repressed under centuries and layers of civilizational ideologies and naturalized, self-mutilations. I can talk with my grandmother; but I can also talk with my refrigerator, washing machine, thermostat, and car ignition, all of which can send me messages and suggestions. At MIT, they are developing a special toilet. Soon even my shit will have something to say.

The body in the olden days of metaphysics was thought to be best instrumentalized by isolation—enforced or self-enforced, natural or naturalized: hermits, monks, Walden Pond, the Rule of St. Benedict, Noble Silence (Buddha), prisons, time-outs, libraries. The Greek philosopher Anaxagoras, who argued that the mind thinks best by itself, epitomizes the view:

> All other things partake in a portion of everything, while *nous* [intelligence and the basis of reason] is infinite and self-ruled, and is mixed with nothing, but is alone, itself by itself. For if it were not by itself, but were mixed with anything else, it would partake in all things if it were mixed with any; . . . things mixed with it would hinder it, so that it would have power over nothing in the same way that it has now being alone by itself.[1]

1. "Anaxagoras: NOUS," Elpenor: Home of the Greek Word, http://

44

The image of the solitary, thinking mind, protecting itself from the ostensible evils of mixture, is finished. Today, the first principle is connection, both in real time and metaphorically. The new Being-Global is saturated with the ethos of connectivity:

Social Connectivity Drives the Engine of Well-Being: Social connections are an essential psychological nutrient.[2]

The number of devices connected to the Internet will top 50 billion by the year 2020. In fact, on average, every person on the globe will have 3.5 connected devices by 2016.[3]

In December 2011, 1.2 billion users worldwide logged on to a social media site.[4] For 2015, the estimate is probably close to 2 billion; 93 percent of the world's adult population are mobile subscribers; 26 percent actively use social networks. But it is *not* the United States that hogs the time on social media! It is Argentina, Mexico, Thailand, the United Arab Emirates, Brazil, South Africa, and Indonesia—in that order. The United States is thirteenth.[5]

But to focus on the expansion of the number of devices is only to fall into the trap of technological progressivism and to debate the merits and demerits of this technology. A better way to approach this is the following: because (in)humans produce opium for the addicted deities, the best use of that opium is to conjoin with them in a hallucinogenic state called connectivity.

Let me step back again.

---

www.ellopos.net/elpenor/greek-texts/ancient-greece/anaxagoras-nous.asp.

2. Christopher Bergland, "Social Connectivity Drives the Engine of Well-Being," *Psychology Today*, May 27, 2013, https://www.psychologytoday.com/blog/the-athletes-way/201305/social-connectivity-drives-the-engine-well-being.

3. John Wagnon, "Security Sidebar: Defending the Internet of Things," DevCentral, March 10, 2014, https://devcentral.f5.com/articles/security-sidebar-defending-the-internet-of-things.

4. José van Dijck, *The Culture of Connectivity: A Critical History of Social Media* (Oxford: Oxford University Press, 2014), 4.

5. "Global Digital Statistics 2014," We Are Social SG, http://www.slideshare.net/wearesocialsg/social-digital-mobile-around-the-world-january-2014.

It is not important that we invented fire but rather what we did around the fire. We cooked, danced, slept, talked, had sex. At some moment—especially after the introduction of agriculture—our social worlds began to be formatted, gendered, textualized, and then theorized and endlessly retheorized. Religions, states, and nations made slaves of some, aristocrats of others, along with merchants, priests, exiles, and nomads. As society became more complex, we narrowed our field of opportunity. We organized society into constitutions and made penal systems. We made governing bodies.

Which brings me to Immanuel Kant, who observed the chaos of the French Revolution from the safety of his German town. "Look this is what happens: chaos, murder, anarchy." And yet, unlike so many others, he did not argue that one should clamp down, bring the royals back, or impose a constitutional mandate. He argued something new by stating categorically that humankind was, at its core, defined by sociability. It required that humans talk to each other over the dinner table, go have coffee together, get to know each other. It was what we would today call a liberal fantasy, but the main point is that, for Kant, there were no law books to publish, no Bibles to thump, and no gospels to print. For the first time in a long time, metaphysics did not require that one first read a text or mumble a sutra, or that one produce and adhere to a text, like a law or contract. It was an astonishing anti-Gutenbergian claim; not just God and king were placed on the backburner but also Descartes's claim that ontology is formed by man's thinking-of-thought. For Kant, the Social was, potentially, at least, open ended.

The argument changed philosophical perspectives in dramatic ways. And indeed, the whole history of philosophy in the nineteenth century tried to grapple with the issue, usually to put a damper on Kant's optimism that things would work out. Hegel, ever nervous, hoped that sociability would congeal into national citizenship. Marx wanted to put it to use to redefine our relationship to labor and create communes of like-minded workers. Kierkegaard hoped that we would all find Christ again. Nonetheless, the nineteenth century saw the gradual opening of the Social. First Jews, then slaves, then women and workers received emancipatory blessings, if more in principle than in fact. Modernist philosophers recoiled and tried to liberate the I from all the surrounding chaos. Nietzsche—disgusted by all the do-goodism—wanted the I to await some magical moment of redemption. Existentialists wanted the I to have her freedom of choice. Other philosophers were more conservative. Dewey emphasized the value of education and art for a stable bourgeoisie. At the far end of the scale, Stalin put people in the gulag. Hitler put people into ovens. Sunnis killed Shi'ites. Fundamentalists wanted Bibles. Gun rights people wanted the Second Amendment.

Being-Global does not proclaim itself victorious over this bizarre landscape of self-righteousness that is at the core of civilization and its multilayered culture of self-hatred. The post-ontological, in the same way that it friends the English language, cohabits the crowded, globalized space of the ontology addicts, deflating them here and there, poking fun at them here and there, reinforcing them here and there. But the new social is not about the Social as such. A Being-Global lives in a technorealist/psychosocial/aesthetic-virtual/contractual-anthropological/postterritorial/data-epistemological/pharma-corrected/playlist-enhanced world. As a result, a Being-Global person is not that concerned with the purity of thought, unless he is a scholar, philosopher, or cognitive scientist. A Being-Global is asked to perform the Social before the Thought, which means that there is no longer any single production of subjectivity that could be extracted from Being and reduced to a moral imperative. Even psychoanalysis has a limited field of operability. Too many variables abound, too many different types of people live in different types of material, social, and cultural conditions:

Using our award winning technologies, including the patented SmartLink, Skyscape coordinates resources for drug information, interactions, clinical information, calculators, tools, clinical trial and research updates. We provide a single point of entry and seamless integration of resources, providing the best user experience for point of care decision support and research needs.[6]

Hi Mark, Someone from India just searched for you on Bing. To see the search query they used and what rank you are on for this query, follow the link below.

6. "All Skyscrape Medical References," Skyscrape, http://www .skyscape.com/estore/ProductDetail.aspx?ProductId=1217.

If philosophers once wanted Being to reflect more deeply on itself—on the "Being-ness of Being" (a *reductio ad absurdum* of the I against the billions of other Is)—post-ontology goes in the other direction. It produces an un-Being-ness of (un)Being, whether purposeful, contractual, or accidental; whether typed in or scanned; whether willing or unwilling. Instead of a light at the end of the tunnel—death and life—we live with thresholds. And once through, once you are an IP address, a download site, the purchaser of an app, a social security number, and so on, any number of potential paths, enforced or unenforced, protected or unprotected, open themselves up to you for communication, solicitation, invasion, and oracular pronouncements. It is a space where things can be true for one person without having to be true for others; and yet all those things form a picture of the (in)human:

> I study the computational basis of human learning and inference. Through a combination of mathematical modeling, computer simulation, and behavioral experiments, I try to uncover the logic behind our everyday inductive leaps: constructing perceptual representations, separating "style" and "content" in perception, learning concepts and words, judging similarity or representativeness, inferring causal connections, noticing coincidences, predicting the future.[7]

The issue is not how the brain works and if it can be effectively modeled by the computer. Let's leave that to cognitive scientists. The issue is that we are fully environmentalized and in essence "housed"—in a split–unsplit algorithmic universe. We live in the differential relations of information gathering. The Rousseauian notion of "I think therefore I am" makes little sense; and on top of that, for every "me," there are millions of insoluble traces of "me"—some more active than others, some more substantial than others—in the digital universe:[8]

> The more content we contribute voluntarily to the public or semi-public corners of the Web, the more we are not only findable, but also knowable.[9]

7. Josh Tenenbaum, http://cocosci.mit.edu/people.

8. John Battelle, "From the Ephemeral to the Eternal," Battelle Media, May 6, 2004, http://battellemedia.com/archives/2004/05/from_the_ephemeral_to _the_eternal.php.

9. Mary Madden, Susannah Fox, Aaron Smith, and Jessica Vitak, "Digital Footprints: Online Identity Management and Search in the Age

Internet users are becoming more aware of their digital footprint; 47% have searched for information about themselves online, up from just 22% five years ago. One in five working American adults (20%) says their employer has a special policy about how employees present themselves online—including what can be shared and posted on blogs and other websites. (2007)[10]

I = onto-engineering + domain axiomatization + I^X.

The new post-ontological Social is no longer oriented around the Troublesome I or the I around the Troublesome Social, both of which are told in the old world to seek reform or improve themselves. The Troublesome I is now part of the Troublesome Social.

The new social is the magical space where—like wine that becomes blood—society receives the beneficence of the (in)human obligation to reveal and conceal.

The student revolutions of 1968 may have unleashed an alternative way of thinking and living for the younger generation of that time, but it was the generation born in the 1970s that blasted ontocentrism out of the water.

1998: Google
1998: PayPal
1999: Netlog
2003: Hi5
2004: Facebook
2004: Flickr
2005: YouTube
2005: Tudou (China)
2005: AfricanZone
2006: Twitter
2006: VK (VKontakte, Russian; literally, "in touch")
2006: Youku (China)
2008: Xt3 (name stands for "Christ in the Third Millennium")
2010: Schtik!

---

of Transparency," Pew Internet and American Life Project, December 6, 2007, http://www.pewinternet.org/files/oldmedia/Files/Reports/2007/PIP _Digital_Footprints.pdf.

10. Ibid.

Being-Global is not the world of the rich. Being-Global is neither the intellectual elite nor the professional intelligentsia. Being-Global is designed to be affordable, the world over. Affordability is the portal into the temple of the gods and the poppy fields of Being:

> Today's field-based mobile workers need to be empowered with the right amount of information at their fingertips to be able to do their jobs better, and more and more enterprises need an affordable solution, especially in emerging markets.[11]

> Facebook users click a "like" button 3 million times a day.[12]

Being-Global lives in a world of contracts, service providers, expiration dates, termination fees, and update protocols. The arrangements are social and contractual, but the result is not the proverbial "social contract" of Locke and Rousseau. I am not giving up my individual freedom to allow others equal freedom. I am producing my *sense* of freedom by binding myself to the realities of (militarized) data capitalism.

At the beginning there was the Word; now there is the Upgrade:

> Foursquare helps you find the perfect places in Belmont to go with friends. [It knows where I live.][13]

There are some who see the new global age as an opportunity for a "progressive world-order sequel." The new social movements "seem at present to embody our best hopes for challenging established and oppressive political, economic, and cultural arrangements at levels of social complexity, from the interpersonal to the international."[14] This by the eminent international law professor Richard A. Falk. Admittedly, he wrote that sentence in 1987, back in the Middle Ages. Today we know better. Globality

11. "A New Level of Affordability," Motorola, http://video.motorolasolutions.com/video.aspx/a-new-level-of-affordability-for-field-mobility-the-mc45-mobile-computer/2096055632001.

12. Viktor Mayer-Schönberger and Kenneth Cukier, *Big Data: A Revolution That Will Transform How We Live, Work, and Think* (New York: Houghton Mifflin Harcourt, 2013), 8.

13. http://www.foursquare.com/.

14. Richard A. Falk, "The Global Promise of Social Movements, Explorations at the Edge of Time," *Alternatives* 12 (1987): 173–96.

hovers around Beings-Global, just as Beings-Global hover over themselves—hover over other versions of themselves.

Augmented virtuality + unvirtual augmentation. Bodies in the Beyond. Beyond Bodies. Bodies in Bodies. Bodies out of Bodies.

Big Data is not the Secondary to Being, the realm of an outside that we can then rationally control through the devices of law and order. It *coexists* with the primacy of Being. And it does so in a way that does not first posit a radical decentering of the subject. The "I" still presumes that it is in possession of the characteristic comprehension—and compression—of itself. The post-ontological I, however, brings to the fore the invisible skein that encoils Being:

Being = Clickstreams.

> Talk about Jedi training! Use the NeuroSky MindWave headset to control this Orbit Helicopter and feel the force flow through your mind. Relax, concentrate and make that baby soar into the sky! On a side note, this little thing looks like a helicopter from Leonardo Da Vinci's time. [$149][15]

Hans-Georg Gadamer, writing in the mid-1960s, desperately tried to find something to hold on to in the nuclear age when the core idea of humanity was being threatened[16]—something to steady ourselves as we move to the uncertain future. "Birth, life, youth, age, native, foreign, determination and freedom. . . . They have measured out what man can plan and what they can achieve."[17] It is an interesting thought, noble for sure, leading supposedly naturally from biology to nation to ideals, but still struggling to link the body with the geo-political premise that Man is tied to some things and yet somehow magically free to seek freedom itself. In today's world, one might be tempted to underline those words. In a world flattened/bloated by globalization, social networks, instant commerce, and Wiland Services, we can no longer focus on the great "measure" of human life. That is for sure.

15. "8 Mind-Blowing Gadgets You Can Control Just with Your Brain," Hongkiat, http://www.hongkiat.com/blog/brain-controlled-gadgets.

16. Hans-Georg Gadamer (1900–2002) was a German philosopher best known for his writing on hermeneutics that attempted to uncover the nature of human understanding.

17. Hans-Georg Gadamer, "Notes on Planning for the Future," *Daedalus* 95, no. 2 (1966): 589.

But read the following from the 2009 Madrid Privacy Declaration, Global Privacy Standards for a Global World: "Warning: that the failure to safeguard privacy jeopardizes associated freedoms, including freedom of expression, freedom of assembly, freedom of access to information, non-discrimination, and ultimately the stability of constitutional democracies."[18] It is typical ontological-survivalist blabber. In the post-ontological world, there is simply no such thing as "freedom of expression." All freedom is monitored and pixilated as data. In fact, the post-ontological world wants nothing more than "freedom of expression." The more people express themselves "freely," the more data will be acquired by the various data deities for whatever purpose they may have.

Theodor Adorno, though he challenged the traditional supremacy of Enlightenment ontology, still believed that "the unity of consciousness is that of the individual human consciousness," and for that reason, so he continues, "the solid, lasting and impermeable side of the 'I' mimics the outside world's impenetrability for consciousness experience."[19] This is old-school thinking. The new equation is something like in Figure 1.

It is not an accident that the Being-Global world posits itself at a time when the nation-state—globally—is under threat (whether through migrations, drugs, terrorism, oppression, fundamentalism, poverty, corruption, ecological mismanagement, natural disasters, wars, etc.). The Being-Global world is not the answer to these ills: it thrives in this context with the support of the great, data-addicted gods who hover over it all with a grin and smirk—Order and Disorder. It keeps the innovations coming.

The situation is sustainable for the simple reason that as computation becomes increasingly democratized, the hack industry will become the leading figure of world politics.

From democracy to hackertocracy. The North Koreans and Chinese have already understood this:

> One of ISIS's more successful ventures is an Arabic-language Twitter app called the Dawn of Glad Tidings, or just Dawn. The app, an

18. "Madrid Declaration," The Public Voice, http://thepublicvoice.org /madrid-declaration.

19. Theodor Adorno, *Negative Dialectics* (New York: Seabury, 1979), 179.

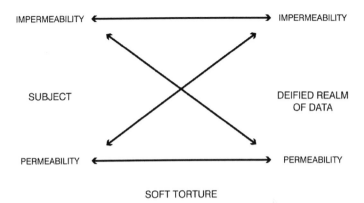

Figure 1. Diagram of the relationship between the realm of the human subject and the realm of data.

official ISIS product promoted by its top users, is advertised as a way to keep up on the latest news about the jihadi group.[20]

The Being-Global world imagines the world differently from the heavy nation-state. It can structure a world against the nation-state—though the nation-state might well be listening in. It can structure a world at the behest of the nation-state, though the advocates of radical liberty might be listening in too. As such, it defines the space of ontological occupation in an increasingly post-nation-state world. It is an infrastructure more robust than any highway. While the highways fall apart, the algorithmic infrastructure is always being rebuilt, updated, refined within days, minutes, microseconds.

The (in)human is constructed on feedback, but because feedback happens at *different* ontological locations and at *different* temporal registers, there is a huge amount of friction. The post-ontological is, therefore, not about the primacy of the feedback loop. The conceit of a sentient, all-knowing computer, of digital intelligence, of a downloadable consciousness, might make for good fiction, but in the post-

20. J. M. Berger, "How ISIS Games Twitter," *The Atlantic*, June 16, 2014, http://www.theatlantic.com/international/archive/2014/06/isis-iraq-twitter-social-media-strategy/372856.

ontological world, this is neither the practice nor the theoretical goal. Yes, its utopian self-projection is to achieve a Bluetoothed universe, but what is really achieved is a world even noisier than a nineteenth-century factory. It is the noise of different scales and dimensions rubbing against each other, denser in some places than in others. It is the noise of images, biologists, comments, vitriol, pornographies, provocations, opinions, texts, and responses. The ocean of mathematics is littered with obsolete codes that bang about in the great ecology of Being, sometimes punching holes in even the sleekest of algorithmic vessels:

> Unfortunately, even with the help of as powerful an instrument as space syntax, there are still hidden analytic dangers lurking just below the surface, especially at the larger scales of analysis.[21]

If the deities of old told us that they made us from clay, at least back then, we were One Thing. Today's polytheistic deities have *no* interest in making us One Thing. We are fashioned out of a wide range of algorithmic languages, some made just a few seconds ago, others hanging around like sleeper cells in our ontological DNA, maybe working, maybe not, maybe waking up one day in a desperate attempt at survival. This algorithmic montage—designed to be invisible on the surface of Being—fakes the attempt to be our seamless companion. And yet, in this approximation, we see ourselves revealed, but only as models, both formed and trapped in a modeled/modeling identity.

Being-Global does not preach about improving ourselves, improving others. That is a question of content. Content and Being have been freely and guiltlessly disconnected for the first time in human history to provide space for the self-militarization of the human/civilian. Being-Global does not proclaim the straight and narrow, nor does it proclaim dissolution. It is not the hated technology of old, the technology that would make us inhuman in the traditional sense of that word. It gives us the opportunity to be as human as we want, depending on how one defines that word. Pornographers played a key role in the development of open content, technically and legally; hackers played a key role

---

21. Bill Hillier, "Can Streets Be Made Safe?," http://www.future communities.net/files/images/CAN_STREETS_BE_MADE_SAFE_1_.pdf.

in exposing bad actors; nation-states operate ceaselessly to create disinformation.

A Being-Global person has no outside—a no-outside without identifiable ideology. A person is called to subjectivity without that call ever taking shape as an outside. The techniques of participation are naturalized too soon, too quickly—now almost at birth. Being-Global in that sense is not political. All politics belong to the spin cycles/gyroscopes of global outflows/inflows. Being-Global is not liberal and not conservative. One "follows." Being-Global is not just living in a personalized community. It is not just participating at some scale or other in a vast chemomathematical industry of cultural production. It produces tribal, national, transnational, communities of its own. Whatever politics you have in all this is potentially embraced in the post-ontological world, yet subject to its various laws of thermodynamics.

The post-ontological does not proclaim itself as avant-garde, as something leading up to change. That myth died with the modernists

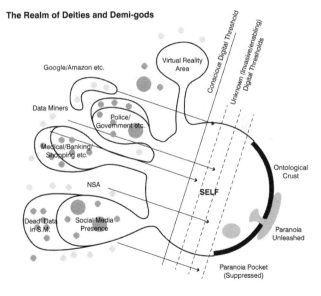

Figure 2. Diagram of the post-ontological condition.

and onto-centric survivors/survivalists/revivalists. Though any individual can play out onto-centric fantasies, we live in a world that is too porous for full epistemic/corporeal/sensate closure.

Being-in-the-world was once all about the struggle for recognition, a struggle theorized and grounded in religion and philosophy. Hegel wanted us to be identified with the State. He wanted us to be National Beings, solid and predictable—good citizens, all. We still live in the moving disaster of that worldview. Derrida wanted to critique this. He called it "deconstruction." But to deconstruct, you need to read—read well—read Plato again and again over a lifetime! Good for him, but it does not scale up.

Being-Global scales up, out, in, and then rescales, or is lost. If there is to be a philosophy from now on, it has to be written in a new language, a language that parodies the old. Being-Global seeks recognition not through ontology as such, not through an academic *discussion* about ontology (philosophers are not needed), not even through a *critique* of ontology (Derrida is not needed), but through friends and networks, through an accumulation of thumbs-ups, downloads, links, and radiational Beings-in-Being.

8. Onto-Paranoia

Charles Barkley is trapped in the Internet and only CDW can save him.

"Why am I in all these places at once? . . . It's OK, they can't see me."

"Yes we can."

—*BUSINESS WIRE* ADVERTISEMENT, 2015

MICHEL FOUCAULT POINTED OUT THAT POWER should not be understood as the classic top-down set of enforcements that produce only an endless supply of unequal relations. Instead, power is a medium that can have different ranges, and in any given instance and place, there are multiple sets of power based on the efficacy of intentionality. Foucault, however, hoped that there was some value to the idea of transgression:

> The play of limits and transgression seems to be regulated by a simple obstinacy: transgression incessantly crosses and recrosses a line which closes up behind it in a wave of extremely short duration, and thus it is made to return once more right to the horizon of the uncrossable.[1]

The modern person, he argued, will never go off to discover a hidden inner truth, as modernism might have hoped, but rath-

---

1. Michel Foucault, "A Preface to Transgression," in *Language, Counter-Memory, Practice: Selected Essays and Interviews*, ed. Donald F. Bouchard, trans. Sherry Simon and Donald F. Bouchard (1963; repr., Ithaca, N.Y.: Cornell University Press, 1980), 34.

er has to try to create a "personal aesthetics of the self." This, he hoped, would shatter the traditional notion of a philosophical subject that was conceived as having an essence that was static and transformable from outside. And while this notion was useful in an older philosophical world, in the new formation, a Being-Global person cannot really locate transgression—nor, for that matter, even ethics.

A Being-Global person lives in a world where transgression is built *into* the system:

I am = I transgress,

You are = You transgress,

He/She is = He/She transgresses,

We are = We transgress,

They are = They transgress,

where "I" refers to individuals, corporations, nations, and even algorithms themselves.

The difficulty, therefore, of sorting truth from falsehood will confound any attempt to study this onto-social space. There is no existential return to ontological security. Many might see this as a symptom of disorder caused by neoliberalism and globalization. Instead, it is a natural part of the safe/dangerous alternative communitarianism that the post-ontological world allows—indeed, requires of us. The very stuff of reality *defines/defies* analysis.

Today, we know that surveillance comes with the territory of being (in)human. The (in)human is surveyed *and* surveyor, both produced *and* producer. Surveillance and production are within the territory of the Human. As a result, the post-ontological condition can sustain/demand different coterminous power relationships. It is a liberatory/carcerated–manufactured/dei-factured world.

Order and disorder are not antithetical. Those very words are archaic. They come from the age of onto-centrism. The algorithmic world seeks to make order out of disorder and disorder out of order. This is what keeps the machinery of empiricism going. Empiricism, once the bedrock of certainty, is now redefined: it is a process that produces disorder to *then* claim to produce order.

THE THIRD LAW OF POST-ONTOLOGICAL THERMODYNAMICS
The more the data-manipulating gods capitalize on order,
the more disorder is purposefully/"accidentally" produced.

The result is a circularity that creates a perpetual, low-intensity torture of the social-civilizational body.

Unlike the era of high fidelity, when it was assumed that engineering could complete the body's sensorial capabilities in a seamless way, the algorithmic world is always designed to grate against ontic surface. The word *flow* is the most inappropriate way to describe this process. That may describe what happens on the electronic side, but to assume that it also describes the ontic side is wrong. There, flow has to be continually disrupted in ever-so-subtle ways so that our relationship to the deities can be repaired, upgraded, reengineered, and recapitalized.

Post-ontology thrives on security threats, real, imagined, fabricated. Security Threat = the Social. Soon *everything* in the world that I need will be the by-product of security. My "I" is a by-product of security.

The data security industry produces *in*security in just the right doses for its self-perpetuation. The system is calculated and legalized in the form of upgrades and contract renewals, patches and defaults, that continuously remind the (in)human—often when he least expects it—of his precarious standing in the social fabric. I call it onto-torture.

In 1996, President Clinton signed the Uniform Trade Secrets Act and the Economic Espionage Act. But we all know that security is a performance economy. Security is there to obscure the fact that the whole purpose is to produce insecurity.

Onto-torture is the only way we can locate our bodies in the hyperoxygenated realm of algorithms. It reminds us, in the form of psychosemiotics, how our senses, even at their most perceptive, cannot fathom the scale of our extended presence. Indeed, our body's senses seem designed not to support life in a fully positive sense but to protect it from a terrifying reality. We live in an algorithmic vivarium with our senses serving as a comforting shield around us.

Even the gods are tortured—tortured by their *own* efforts, because they, too, have to monitor themselves, monitor their mathematical foundations to either extract more information out of the data or protect themselves from those who see gaps and lacunae and thus aim to seize an opportunity in remodeling their systems. The gods want *their* "privacy" as best they can achieve it.

The informal economy of insecurity as a side effect has now become an economy in its own right: the (in)security economy.

One way not to say "structural disruption" is to say "innovation." And what is the source of all of this innovation? The appropriately anonymous authors of Wikipedia state it quite well: "it can occur as a result of a focus effort by a range of different agents, by chance, or as a result of a major system failure."[2] Lovely! We need more system failures! Big screw-ups are not really screw-ups. The gods will provide . . . more humans who will always screw up.

As data providers, we are by definition prone to mistakes. It is in fact required of us, and not just to make mistakes but to fail to understand the very nature of transgression:

> Personal details of Obama, Putin, Cameron and Merkel accidentally leaked by G20 summit organiser in privacy breach. The cause of the breach was human error. [Redacted] failed to check that the autofill function in Microsoft Outlook had entered the correct person's details into the email "To" field. This led to the email being sent to the wrong person.[3]

> The initial investigations in the US have shown that the "technical glitch" at NYSE was caused by some "internal software upgrade" and the regulators and other agencies have so far ruled out any external reasons such as cyber attacks.[4]

> Banks Generate $30bn of Abusive Overdraft Fees[5]

2. Wikipedia, s.v. "Innovation," http://en.wikipedia.org/wiki/Innovation.

3. Lucy Clarke-Billings, "Personal Details of Obama, Putin, Cameron and Merkel Are Accidentally Leaked by G20 Summit Organiser in Privacy Breach," *The Independent,* March 30, 2015, http://www.independent.co.uk /news/world/personal-details-of-obama-putin-cameron-and-merkel-sent -to-wrong-email-address-by-g20-summit-organiser-10142539.html.

4. "NYSE Halt: Sebi, Exchanges Review Risk Management Systems," *India Times,* July 9, 2015, http://economictimes.indiatimes.com/markets /stocks/news/nyse-halt-sebi-exchanges-review-risk-management-systems /articleshow/48003253.cms.

5. Nick Clements, "Banks Generate $30bn of Abusive Overdraft Fees,"

Banks Making the Most from Overdraft and ATM Fees[6]

This torture has words like progress, innovation, regulation, de-regulation, scam, scam protection, net neutrality, data protection, and so on. Glitch. Crash. Zero day vulnerability. Packet injection—a great vectoral mash-up designed to simultaneously mitigate *and* multiply this torture that is usually accidental or unprecedented:

> Make sure that you follow these steps carefully. For added protection, back up the registry before you modify it. Then, you can restore the registry if a problem occurs. For more information about how to back up and restore the registry, click the following article number to view the article in the Microsoft Knowledge Base.[7]

When a system fails, if a problem occurs, it is not that the system really fails; it means that the system is working! Each of us is a living, breathing system failure. When our computer crashes, we must remember that it is designed to crash. The same for the world economy; it is the foundation of data volume capitalism:

> Zuckerberg's Facebook page hacked to prove security flaw.[8]

> "Oops: This webpage is not available."[9]

> Language packs are no longer available after you upgrade to Windows 8.1 from Windows 8.[10]

> Zero day worms take advantage of a surprise attack while they are unknown to computer security professionals. Recent history shows

---

Magnify Money, June 17, 2015, http://www.magnifymoney.com/blog/consumer-watchdog/banks-generate-30bn-abusive-overdraft-fees831289452.

6. John C. Ogg, "Banks Making the Most from Overdraft and ATM Fees," 24/7 Wall St., June 17, 2015, http://247wallst.com/banking-finance/2015/06/17/banks-making-the-most-from-overdraft-and-atm-fees.

7. "Support for Windows Server 2003," Microsoft, http://support.microsoft.com/kB/282402.

8. Doug Gross, "Zuckerberg's Facebook Page Hacked to Prove Security Flaw," CNN, August 20, 2013, http://www.cnn.com/2013/08/19/tech/social-media/zuckerberg-facebook-hack.

9. Network errors 2, 101, 102, 104, 105, and 324.

10. "Support for Windows Language Packs," Microsoft, https://support.microsoft.com/en-us/kb/2910256.

an increasing rate of worm propagation. Well-designed worms can spread within minutes (some say even seconds) with devastating consequences to Internet and otherwise.[11]

RedSeal software creates maps of networks, and then conducts fire drills with dummy viruses and other malware to see where potential holes are, as well as the likely migration path of system threats once they've been discovered.[12]

UK airspace shutdown caused by unprecedented computer glitch[13]

Encryption protocols; crypto management; bitlockers; tripwires; optimization packs. "Can't access your account? Sign in here to a secure site." (Good luck!)

The algorithmic universe compresses into a single force the traditionally competing tendencies of devitalization and vitalization. Old-school metaphysics—the metaphysics of religion, for example—separated these, where the first, with its doctrines of shame, humiliation, and otherness, was little more than the leverage toward the second. The post-ontological world does not change this per se, except that it operates at a reduced and more sophisticated level, namely, at the more human scale. For example, our humiliation at the hands of data providers who want to render us predictable and understandable is couched as necessary for our protection, if not for our existence:

The reimagined Samsung Galaxy Note5 is designed to keep up with your busy life.[14]

Algorithmic vortexes stand halfway between something like gravity, which we have completely naturalized without consciously noticing, and evolution, which, regardless of how we might accept it, will

11. Wikipedia, s.v. "Zero Day," https://en.wikipedia.org/wiki/Zero-day _(computing).

12. Jeremy Quittner, "Why Some Small Businesses Love Hack Attacks," *Inc.*, October 7, 2014, http://www.inc.com/jeremy-quittner/following-chase -break-in-small-businesses-fight-back.html.

13. Danica Kirka, "U.K. Airspace Shutdown Caused by Unprecedented Computer Glitch," *Toronto Star*, December 13, 2014, http://www.thestar.com /news/world/2014/12/13/uk_airspace_shutdown_caused_by_unprecedented _computer_glitch.html.

14. "The New Gold Standard," Verizon Wireless, http://www.verizonwireless.com /landingpages/samsung/?gclid=COHGprTz9MoCFQV4NwodGiYH8g&gclsrc=ds.

never be naturalized either individually or globally. The algorithmic I slides between these extremes and is designed that way. We must continually build, secure, and then rebuild and resecure our ontic world.

The *more* data, the *greater* the addiction by the data deities, the *more* disruption is required. But these disruptions have to be fed into the system in precise amounts. The results can never dehumanize us completely, or else the great deities that produce the algorithms would face a backlash that can easily "go viral"—such as when we discovered that Samsung televisions could possibly spy on our conversations. The results can never be so much in debate that entire communities reject them. Like a pendulum, they correct and self-correct. The steady state is a dynamic one. We expect that the iPhone will be updated every year or so, but not every month.

Being a (in)human is to be a beta tester.

Risk in the post-ontological world is continually at play. It is enhanced to an integral part of life but is mitigated to continually produce a dependency relationship. A touch of a screen brings the fire truck or police. An automatic sensor in our phone beeps if it detects certain chemicals. Our cars stop before a crash. Driver safety classes will soon no longer be needed.

The embarrassment to the government caused by Snowden compensates for the invisible intrusions foisted on (in)humans. Justice is detached from perpetrator.

Since 2005—the birth of the so-called Social Media Age—background checks on people wanting to buy guns have risen from fewer than 10 million per year to close to 20 million in 2014. Is it only because of the activities of the NRA and school shootings? Or is there a deeper cause, namely, the parallelism between the "militarization" of a population (i.e., the rise of social media) and its upstream militarization?

A Being-Global person is a threat alert; high or low depends on the nature of the data exhaust. We become suspect when we produce not enough onto-exhaust or too much, when algorithms start to fail to connect the dots, or when the dots fail to match up with predictions. The rest of us are positioned by the cumulative efforts of the deities to inhabit a steady state zone, the active zone that produces the most useful data.

Some people reach a tipping point. They throw their cell phones into the fountain. Tear up their Verizon contracts. Jab at their screens. Say nasty things. The onto-torture has reached a tipping point. This is not good for the civilianization complex.

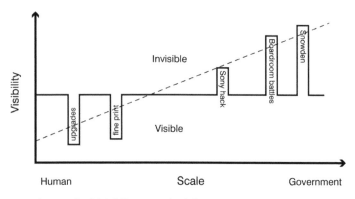

Figure 3. The (in)visibility penetration index.

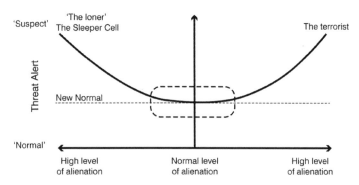

Figure 4. The desired steady state alert index for the civilianized population.

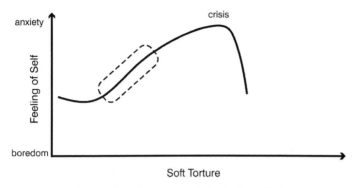

Figure 5. The desired steady state torture index for the civilianized population.

We lose faith in the instruments that produce our onto-exhaust. "Just enough" torture is now considered normal. By preserving us in that realm, the outliers are more easily visible, the sleeper cells and the terrorists.

The warmth of the participatory ethos (music, shopping, travel) softens the pain. At the level of the deities, it is profit extraction (for the likes of Bill Gates, for example) that softens the pain, and at the national level, it is the busywork of passing laws and the occasional making of arrests:

1984: Comprehensive Crime Control Act

1986: Computer Fraud and Abuse Act

1990: Operation Sundevil: crackdown on "illegal" computer hacking

1996: Telecommunications Act

2001: USA PATRIOT Act

2004: Computer-Assisted Passenger Pre-screening System (CAPPS)

2007: PRISM: a clandestine antiterrorism mass electronic surveillance data-mining program

To further soften the torture, the architects of the digital world have devised a new discipline, data visualization. We can see ourselves, our politics, our loves and hates. We are told that we can learn something from this—make "improvements" to this or that—even to ourselves.

Data visualization is the Digital Stockholm Syndrome.

It is a paradox that "our self-aestheticizing performance as subjects . . . feeds into our ever more precise (self-)identification as knowable and predictable (in)human–digital objects."[15] But self-aestheticizing is only *half* of the equation at best. After all, an algorithm is an aesthetic too:

1990: The first Institute of Electrical and Electronics Engineers Visualization Conference[16]

Since 2005, some public-access visualization sites:

WeFeelFine.org

Betterworldflux.com

Visual.ly

dipity.com

We Feel Fine.org harvests human feelings . . . from many weblogs. Every few minutes, the system searches the world's newly posted blogs for the phrases "I feel" and "I am feeling." When it finds such a phrase, it records the full sentence, up to the period, and identifies the "feeling" expressed in that sentence (e.g., sad, happy, depressed). Because blogs are structured in largely standard ways, the age, gender, and geographical location of the author can often be extracted and saved, as can the local weather conditions when the sentence was written. As you click anywhere on the screen, flying balls of information will scatter about. If you scroll over one of them, it'll provide a bit more detail, and clicking will open a new page.[17]

Being-Global represses the terror of indeterminacy, which is voided—avoided—by the pleasure of the circulating, gaseous-fluid substance of sociality. Being-Global accepts the soft torture of indeterminacy—the information life cycle. The pharma establishment softens the pain.

---

15. Robert Craig, "Dilthey, Gadamer, and Facebook: Towards a New Hermeneutics of the Social Network," *Modern Language Review* 110, no. 1 (2015): 185.

16. Jonathan Harris and Sepandar Kamvar, "Mission," IEE Explore, May 2006, http://ieeexplore.ieee.org/xpl/mostRecentIssue.jsp?punumber=311.

17. "Mission," We Feel Fine, http://wefeelfine.org/mission.html.

The U.S. Federal Drug Administration (FDA) in 1977 enabled pharmaceutical companies to more easily advertise to the public. Then, in 1997, the Draft Guidance for Industry: Consumer-Directed Broadcast Advertisements outlined the ways in which pharmaceutical manufacturers could advertise on television. Let's call it the "civilianization of medicine." Since then, spending on direct-to-consumer ads has nearly quadrupled. In 2011, the pharmaceutical and medical device industries provided 32% of all funding for continuing medical education courses in the United States—$752 million out of $2.35 billion.

Is it an accident that nearly one in four women ages 50 to 64 in the U.S. were found to be on an antidepressant, with 13 percent of the overall population also on antidepressants . . . 13 percent were on painkilling opioids?[18]

One hundred thousand Americans die each year from prescription drugs. That's 270 per day—more than twice as many people as are killed in car accidents each day.[19]

1998: Jeffrey Arnold launches WebMD, an Internet portal for health and medical information, used now by over 40 million people each month.

"Pharma companies want to add an app to your next prescription."[20]

The post-ontological world lives in a circulatory system of

Problem–solution: solution produces new "problem"

Illness–cure: cure produces new "illness"

Need–innovation: innovation produces new "need"

Danger–resolution: resolution produces new "danger"

Privacy–breach: more "privacy"

18. "Study Shows 70 Percent of Americans Take Prescription Drugs," CBS News, June 20, 2013, http://www.cbsnews.com/news/study-shows-70 -percent-of-americans-take-prescription-drugs.

19. Daniela Perdomo, "100,000 Americans Die Each Year from Prescription Drugs, While Pharma Companies Get Rich," Alternet, June 24, 2010, http://www.alternet.org/story/147318/100,000_americans_die_each _year_from_prescription_drugs,_while_pharma_companies_get_rich.

20. Satish Misra, "Pharmacompanies Want to Add an App at Your Next Prescription," iMedicalApps, December 18, 2014, http://www.imedicalapps .com/2014/12/pharma-companies-want-add-app-next-prescription.

What neurosis was for modernists, paranoia is for post-ontologists:

> Paranoia on the rise, experts say.[21]
>
> Report: Emerging Culture of Paranoia.[22]
>
> "Patriot" Paranoia: A Look at the Top Ten Conspiracy Theories.[23]
>
> Comment: The rise of paranoia in British politics[24]
>
> Your Paranoia Is Real[25]
>
> *Paranoia* (the movie)[26]
>
> Study: Paranoia on the Rise, Those Afflicted Feel Persecution and Rejection[27]

For modernists, paranoia was caused by latent homosexuality (Freud), childhood abuse, coddling, or a cognitive empathy deficit (!). That will soon change. Paranoia will be normalized. Like looking for a cure to cancer, we will invest heavily in solving the problem of paranoia, while continuing to do things that promote it. "Cyber Crime Costs $114B per Year."[28] Great! There is already a

---

21. "Paranoia on the Rise," *Las Vegas Sun,* November 12, 2008, http://www.lasvegassun.com/news/2008/nov/12/paranoia-on-the-rise-experts-say.

22. Tom Allison, Marcia Kuntz, and Raphael Schweber-Koren, "Emerging Culture of Paranoia: Obama Derangement Syndrome Epidemic on Conservative Airwaves," Media Matters, April 13, 2009, http://mediamatters.org/research/2009/04/13/report-emerging-culture-of-paranoia/149126.

23. Alexander Zaitchik, "'Patriot' Paranoia: A Look at the Top Ten Conspiracy Theories," *Intelligence Report* 139 (Fall 2010), http://www.splcenter.org/get-informed/intelligence-report/browse-all-issues/2010/fall/patriot-paranoia.

24. Matthew Ashton, "The Rise of Paranoia in British Politics," Politics.co.uk, November 13, 2011, http://www.politics.co.uk/comment-analysis/2011/11/13/comment-the-rise-of-paranoia-in-british-politics.

25. Ben Cosgrove, "Your Paranoia Is Real," *Time,* July 17, 2012, http://entertainment.time.com/2012/07/18/13-worst-ever-movie-taglines-inspired-by-the-dark-knights-stinker/slide/your-paranoia-is-real.

26. http://www.imdb.com/title/tt1413495/combined.

27. "Study: Paranoia on the Rise, Those Afflicted Feel Persecution and Rejection," CBS Washington, D.C., June 14, 2013, http://washington.cbslocal.com/2013/06/14/study-paranoia-on-the-rise-those-afflicted-feel-persecution-rejection.

28. Cloe Albanesius, "Cyber Crime Costs $114B per Year, Mobile Attacks

booming market in paranoia. The Blackphone is purpose-built for the post-Snowden era: it encrypts all of a user's data and comes preloaded with apps designed with secrecy in mind, to block "information leakage."[29]

From one perspective, paranoia is the shadow of Big Data and its deities on our consciousness. From another perspective, it is its very illumination.

Paranoia is no longer the psychoanalytical problem but is more like a virus that lives in the (in)human host on a continual basis, even though it may not be apparent in daily life. For some people, it manifests on the surface of existence to allow Being to see the microgeopolitics of desire. The result is an oracular positioning vis-à-vis the great deities. Whether we pay attention to such oracles depends on our capacity to listen to hallucinated voices.

Paranoia is not a symptom that needs to be cured, even though we will continue to operate in those standard modernist terms. It is the operating system (in the computational sense of functions needed to control and synchronize a computer's activities). But unlike OSes in my computer, paranoia is biologically based, and thus its normalization has to be produced internally to the needs and desires of life itself. Biology does not work, in other words, with "upgrades." Upgrades are not the actual cause of paranoia—though it may seem that way—but the external modifiers of a paranoidic technology that must deny the crisis of potential collapse. Paranoia is the key requirement of this biotechnical process. It is the blood system that keeps the three post-ontological, thermodynamical equations in play.

It is no accident of history that the normalization of paranoia coincides with the legalization of marijuana in the United States. Hallucinogens were common among first societies as a means to better listen and speak to the deities. For us, they delegitimize monotheistic allegiance to the singularity of the text. They help us "see" the psychedelic imaginaries of equations and power, imaginaries that are governed by deities who are themselves addicted to our ontic exhaust.

on the Rise," *PCMag,* September 11, 2011, http://www.pcmag.com/article2/0,2817,2392570,00.asp.

29. Richard Waters, "Privacy Boom Brings Digital Paranoia into the Open," *Financial Times,* July 3, 2014, http://www.ft.com/cms/s/0/f970d000-0291-11e4-a68d-00144feab7de.html#axzz3PxhgjFEC.

An ontological crust, a place where our traditional sense of identity toward the outside condenses, contains our sense-of-Self. This crust can be loose, flexible, even compliant, or it can harden into identity politics and fundamentalism. This onto-crust is fed just as much from the outside (as in standard encounters with other (in)humans) as it is from the inside. Inside: not as in desire and passions—the interiorities of old—but as the known/unknown organization of energies that infuses its prerogatives into our sense of Being.

Our onto-crust interfaces between the digital habitat and the conventional one. It is the container of the traditional Self. It can be partially detached from the technology of devices, should the Self want, but it can never be immune from the actions of the deities. If you disconnect, woe be to you. In France, if you stop eating baguettes, you might now be seen to be on the path to terrorism.

It would be wrong to think that the onto-crust is just the meek residue of a former Self. Our onto-crust hooks itself into the flesh of the digital, draining energy from it, for its psychic purposes. Paranoia rests below the surface of the onto-crust. The harder the crust gets, the more likely it will fissure, allowing paranoia to leak out. Flowing to the surface, paranoia spreads out over us, defining us. It is no longer an illness but the everyday, the everywhere.

Music is designed to soften the ontological crust; it socializes us on the exterior and interior. Favorites, playlists, Shazam, iTunes, podcasts, albums, artists. We are all walking, eating, running, pissing, shitting digital DJs. Listening to music everywhere, anywhere.

Music is an onto-sphere unto itself, with digital sounds entering the ear in return for a wealth of digital onto-bits that tag us, mark us, identify us in myriad ways. Music is designed to saturate the onto-crust. It is the new metaphysics. Music molds our ontology, prepares it, protomilitarizes it.

The onto-crust exists in the time zone of life. The onto-bits, by way of contrast, live in a technoelectronic hypertemporality; each is pegged to a specific time, down to a fraction of a second as registered by an atomic clock. They are not frozen in time; rather, each is an x-y-z punctum in a great temporal fog. (GPS satellites have on board at least two cesium and as many as two rubidium atomic clocks. The relative times are mathematically transformed into three absolute spatial coordinates and one absolute time coordinate. The time is accurate to within approximately fifty nanoseconds.) From ontology to trackology.

The data deities share this paranoia with us. Our paranoia is just the corporeal *metaphor* for a substance that, like oil, smooths the operations of a post-ontological life.

Mind/paranoia: they are the same word!

Mind [*nous*] = Paranoia [παρά (*para*), "beside, by" + (*nous*)]

1972: *The End of Philosophy* by Martin Heidegger is translated from German to English. The end, indeed!

2012: "Rogue algorithm" causes havoc on the New York Stock Exchange.

2013: "Being suspicious is good."[30]

2014: "New Algorithms Search for Signs of Consciousness in Brain Injury Patients"[31]

Paranoia is a structural part of the give-and-take with what we might still call "reality," the goo that holds everything together, the warm host for the algorithmic microbes.

When we die—when our onto-crust disappears—we leave behind a cubist portrait of onto-shadows.

---

30. "A Healthy Digital Paranoia," Internet Safety Project, https://www.internetsafetyproject.org/wiki/healthy-digital-paranoia.

31. Greg Miller, "New Algorithms Search for Signs of Consciousness in Brain Injury Patients," *WIRED*, October 16, 2014, http://www.wired.com/2014/10/neural-signature-consciousness.

The Three Laws of Post-Ontological Thermodynamics

THE FIRST LAW
The physical system (of data) = natural system = human system

THE SECOND LAW
"data" = data surplus > data processing

THE THIRD LAW
The more the data manipulating gods capitalize on order, the more disorder is purposefully/"accidentally" produced.

Afterword
Onto-Tecture

IN THE MID-1960S, intellectuals in the architectural community hoped that the time was ripe to humanize buildings and make them more suited to the construction of positive experiences. The new field was called architectural psychology. Astonishingly, by the mid-1980s, the field had begun to disappear. It was replaced by questions of how to *use* psychology to manipulate humans in space. Book publication dates chart the changing disciplinary environment with crystal clarity. The year 1999 is when we "enter" the mind of the shopper. This shopper is no longer the classic "human" but a data set. From then on, it is only a matter of time before profits and happiness can both be delivered:

1974: *Graphic Display of Human Behavior: Environment Data with an Emphasis on Institutional Setting*

1974: *Psychology and the Built Environment*

1974: *Psychology for Architects*

1975: *Architecture and Awareness of Self*

1977: *Environment and Behavior: Planning and Everyday Urban Life*

1977: *People, Paths, and Purpose: Notations for a Participatory Environtecture*

1980: *A Psychology of Building: How We Shape and Experience Our Structured Spaces*

1983: *K. Pardo and Remy Landau patent granted*

1986: *Principles of Data Mining and Knowledge Discovery (First European Conference)*

1986: *Designing to Sell: A Complete Guide to Retail Store Planning and Design*

1995: *Time-Saver Details for Store Planning and Design*

1999: *Inside the Mind of the Shopper: The Science of Retailing*

1999: *Why We Buy: The Science of Shopping*

2003: *The Ten Demandments: Rules to Live by in the Age of the Demanding Customer*

2010: *Delivering Happiness: A Path to Profits, Passion, and Purpose*

2011: *What Women Want: The Science of Female Shopping*

In this world where the human has thrown off its gravitational sensibility, we have learned how excellent we are at playing human within the swirl of algorithmic fantasies. There are no creators in the classical sense; thus our fascination with its replacement, innovators—those magical creatures that serve as culture's battery packs. To honor them, we produce innovation communities[1] and innovation districts: Atlanta, Baltimore, Barcelona, Berlin, Boston, Buffalo, Cambridge, Cleveland, Detroit, Houston, London, Medellin, Montreal, Providence, San Francisco, Seattle, Seoul, Stockholm, Toronto, and so on. Innovation drivers, innovation cultivators, innovation ecosystems:

> Innovation districts have the unique potential to spur productive, inclusive and sustainable economic development. At a time of sluggish growth, they provide a strong foundation for the creation and expansion of firms and jobs by helping companies, entrepreneurs, universities, researchers and investors—across sectors and disciplines—co-invent and co-produce new discoveries for the market.[2]

That, at least, is the story.

In the meantime, waiting to see if any of this is true, we live in the quaint huts of our ontologically enforced—ontologically reinforced—archaic past. We live in ticky-tacky houses, ticky-tacky high-rise apartments, ticky-tacky appliances, ticky-tacky slums. Like snails, we carry our precious traditions and cultural conformism everywhere we go, squeezing buildings out into the landscape like toothpaste. No one objects. We are mute. We do not really care. The construction industry is just another god in the

---

1. Richard Florida, *The Rise of the Creative Class* (New York: Basic Books, 2002).

2. Bruce Katz and Julie Wagner, "The Rise of Innovation Districts," Brookings Metropolitan Policy Program, May 2014, http://www.brookings.edu/~/media/Programs/metro/Images/Innovation/InnovationDistricts1.pdf.

Great Pantheon of beings churning up the earth in the name of jobs and progress.

The Dutch architect Rem Koolhaas calls what we see when we look out of the window "junk space." And indeed, there is reciprocity between junk space and post-ontological space. Both feed on the population boom—on the surfeit of buildings and humans in the world. Both avoid the middle ground of reality, while promising endlessly to change and improve it.

The disparity between how we live in our houses and how we operate as a Being-Global is no longer seen as bizarre. It is the New Natural. The post-ontological does not ask for some radical avant-garde. On the contrary, it is like a vast preservation machine. It likes conformity and predictability. Data, after all, is a product of the predictable.

Let the contractors have junk space. The innovation industry will upgrade it with smart sensors:

> No more turning the phone to landscape to set your thermostat to Away or check Energy History. Just tap the three line icon at the top right, or swipe the whole screen to the left, and you'll see your schedule, settings, everything you need.[3]

The post-ontological is a type of *preservation machine* that keep atavisms continually in play. Preservation, as a field in architecture, developed in the 1970s and escalated rapidly in the following decades into an established field with powerful footprints in politics, culture, and urbanism. This global naturalization of preservation has more to do with understanding the balance of power between Being and Global than with the supposed promises and associated anxieties having to do with computer and computational intelligence. Basically, in the post-ontological age, the more stable certain things are, the more they can be rendered into predictable, but frictional, data-producing entities. So the mythology of innovation that many swallow without a thought is in reality often preservational in nature. Just think of Wikipedia. Though it can be updated, many entries are already virtually locked up forever, mistakes and all. Hospital and police records can be just as

---

3. E-mail sent to me from my thermostat.

secure in their longevity as any medieval manuscript! Just as architectural preservation keeps buildings alive and restored in a bubble of time well past their identification with contemporary culture, post-ontology preserves ontology as its prime mechanism for data production:

> The General Conference adopted Resolution 34 at its 31st session, drawing attention to the ever-growing digital heritage in the world and the need for an international campaign to safeguard endangered digital memory.[4]

So let Zaera-Polo complain about the "homogenization of urban topographies" and how liquid economy "disintegrates the urban body."[5] Such thoughts imply the classic image of ontocentrism, allowing Zaera-Polo to reinforce the classic idea of body = architecture, or, in his words, "like the skin of a living creature, the envelope [of a building] is the primary actor."[6] But in a post-ontological world, there is no such thing as "skin," largely because "body" is itself an ambiguous proposition.

A global, device-oriented, chemo-corrected, post-ontological people no longer need the intensity-of-contemporaneity that modern architecture or even contemporary art could provide— or tries to provide. We are happy with the standard look, even though contemporary art and architecture can try to *perform* the question of the anxiety-of-the-subject. But in the meantime, the city has become more predictable and easier to plan than ever before:

> Now the home security and automation platform is finally ready for prime time. . . . The most powerful feature, though, is the ability to create programs that can automate tasks, send alerts and trigger events based on data from the sensors. For example, if the glass break sensor on the kitchen window is tripped, the system can be set to turn on the lights in the room and start recording a video.

4. Colin Webb, "Guidelines for the Preservation of Digital Heritage," UNESCO, March 2003, http://unesdoc.unesco.org/images/0013/001300 /130071e.pdf.

5. Alejandro Zaera-Polo, *The Sniper's Log: Architectural Chronicles of Generation-X,* ed. Gavin Keeney (Princeton, N.J.: Princeton School of Architecture, 2012), 30–31.

6. Ibid., 481.

Eventually, AT&T even sees the ability to integrate with the location services on a cellphone for additional automation options.[7]

But remember that just as the security industry designs security to periodically fail, thus our fascination with urban terror, urban planning is designed to fail as well and thus to always place the blame on others. I am, therefore, not interested in celebrating the smooth, ostensibly mediated world of information and digital visualization. We can easily create a space, for example, that "is infused with information that seeds the production and conveyance of experience and meaning."[8] Some architects argue that our newly found data capacity allows buildings to be more responsive and even more responsible. Although this may have some merit, my point is to focus past the lure of what architecture can do in this new condition. "Mediated architecture" will not show our inner thoughts, our police records, our family backgrounds, our voting records, and so forth. It restricts itself ever so politely to the rather predictable sensate/psychological needs of human–building interaction. In that sense, like the cultural project known as "entertainment," its main purpose is more to suck information out of us than to reveal to us anything deep about our social world:

Such spaces might speak to our yearning for progressivism and avant-gardism, but they do not remove Being from the yaw of a monotheist, anthrocentric singularity. A digital sensorium only gives more credence to an imaginary human destiny that is wrapped up in the illusion of its own ostensible immanence.

One can, of course, find any number of creative artists who tackle the question of human/digital/memory. Take Eduard Kac, whose work encompasses many genres and fields: holography, works to be transmitted by fax, photocopied art, experimental photography, video, fractals, digital art, microchips approached as human prostheses, virtual reality, networks, robotics, satellites, telerobotics, teletransportation, genomes, biotechnology,

7. Terrence O'Brien, "AT&T Launches Digital Life Home Automation and Security Platform," April 26, 2013, http://www.engadget.com/2013/04/26/atandt-launches-digital-life-home-automation-and-security-platform.

8. Johan Bettum, "The Theatre of Immanence," *SAC Journal 2: Mediated Architecture*, Spring 2015, 15.

Morse code, DNA.[9] For one of his artworks, *Time Capsule* (1997), he implanted a microchip in his ankle, "an area of the body that has been traditionally chained or branded."[10] Surrounded by 1930s photographs of his grandmother's family, who were annihilated in Poland during World War II, he then scanned his body to register it with a U.S. databank via the Internet to create himself as a vehicle for cultural memory and a locus of historical inscription. Just as the chip is inserted in his body, he inserts his data into the system to speak of loss and presence, the real and the virtual.

Another artist is Rafael Lozano-Hemmer. His *Please Empty Your Pockets* (2003) consists of a computer-controlled scanner and an airport-type conveyor belt. Museumgoers place an item of their choice on the conveyor belt; scanned images of it are presented with others retrieved from a database of six hundred thousand items scanned during the installation.[11]

Artists like this are far ahead of the game compared to architecture, which is generally locked into a world of digital utopianism built at best around the limitations of digital design that celebrate bioresponsive wall surfaces; table projections; and computer-generated, biomorphic forms. So the question remains open as to whether a new design has to be a critical reflection of our current condition or whether architecture is too stubborn a discipline and too dependent on social approvals and technological optimism ever to capture the possibilities of our age. By the standards of the art world, the answer would have to be yes; but by the standards of post-ontology, what is meant by "critical" must also be left open. *Critical* is just another signifier of the anthrocentric, Enlightenment project. A post-ontological everyday can have components that can, at best, play the part of a critique.

We would certainly have to tackle the question of how our onto-bits are vacuumed up, digested, and reconstituted. We

9. Ángel Kalenberg, "Eduardo Kac: The Artist as Demiurge," *ArtNexus Guide 69*, June–August 2008, http://www.artnexus.com/Notice_View.aspx?DocumentID=19376.

10. Eduardo Kac, *Teleporting an Unknown State* (Slovenia: KIBLA, 1998), 49, 51.

11. Rafael Lozano-Hemmer, "Please Empty Your Pockets," http://www.lozano-hemmer.com/please_empty_your_pockets.php.

would have to deal with the question of our status of (in)human/ civilians enmeshed in the naturalized, (self-)militarization of the data/security economy. But above all, post-ontological design would have to exist in the *frictional* gap between location and dislocation. What, then, is the spatial/despatial geography of the post-ontological?

THE ELEMENTS OF ONTO-TECTURE

Paranoia Pod: It has two rooms, with a single door for each. One room is a "dark space" and lined with lead to prevent surveillance. The other is fitted out with all the necessary plug-ins and screens for surveillance, hidden cams, motion detectors, and heat sensors. Paranoia Pods is heavily advertised on Fox TV and MSNBC. The pods are available through Paranoia Construction Inc.

Onto-deck: Here one can reground oneself in the illusory Being-ness of Being, with the assumption that how one "stands" on the surface indicates one's ontological leaning. The surface can be pine needles to give a sense of standing in a Heideggerian forest. It can be sand to give a sense of beach and ocean. Or it can be concrete to give a sense of foundation. The lighting and acoustic conditions will be designed to replicate the appropriate environment. Each person to her own, the architect will provide. Onto-Deck Inc. will send its representatives to your house for a free consultation.

Beheard.org: There is nothing more potent in our semiotically deprived world than the yard sign, a physical and spatial device of communication. Have your thoughts expressed at low cost and broadcast to your community from the legal safety of your yard. Signs are painted on aluminum or wood and in weather-resistant paints. They will be delivered the day following payment. For a special price, we can install your sign on your roof so that your words can be visible from Google Earth.

Onto-gorithm-screen (OGS): An algorithm designed to scout for onto-bits projects its information on a large screen. The display is designed to give the owner continuous updates on where one's onto-bit information is housed. It does automatic searches and has a large, digital dial that estimates the proportion of visible to invisible data. It has suggestions on how to either increase or decrease that proportion. Best Buy is the seller and custom installer for the OGS.

Personalized fog device (PFG): What if you and I, instead of providing the algorithmic deities the billions of onto-bits of real data—

for free!—provide billions of data bits of fictional data? You cannot create false bank accounts and the like without going to jail, but you can flood the servers with false activity. You could hire someone to click on random sites when you are away from the computer, but better yet, you could purchase a personalized fog device (PFG), known generally as a fogger, that you plug into any computer and that sends out false information. The device can be customized to send out particular types of information and at various speeds and in any language. You can even customize a range of personalities. Its programs are continually kept up to date to conform to local and federal laws and regulations. One hundred percent safe, this is the best way to get back at those who steal, mine, and thrive data that is taken from us. Join the millions of users who are already confounding the data miners! The basic PFG can be purchased online for $10.58. The more advanced PFG that can Bluetooth to other, similar devices costs $24.86.

Onto-port: Doors have scanning devices that register one's presence and send tweets and e-mails to a set list of people ("Hi, Mom, I am in the kitchen"). Onto-door is programmed to locate mittens, scarves, socks, and other things, because all clothing—and, indeed, all items—are now traceable. Several features are optional, including a sustainability button that evaluates your possessions and purchases in regard to their carbon footprint and compares them with your neighbors' purchases. (Warning: an unconfirmed rumor has been spread that a hidden algorithm sends information to the police and IRS.) Another feature allows you to send arbitrary photos from your personal archive to the FBI or to any other large data-analytic entity for storage, depending on the settings, to produce false positives and to fog over your presence. A special feature will change your facial features in any way that you want.

These doors, marketed through Home Depot, are simple for any electrician to install and are a great gift idea, depending on how many doors one has in a house. A starter package consists of two onto-ports.

Annotations

Introduction

Kant is here elaborating a point of view first developed, though in different contexts, by Spinoza. Spinoza argued that "both the decision of the mind and the appetites and the determination of the body by nature exist together—or rather are one and the same thing, which we call a decision when it is considered under, and explained through, the attribute of thought, and which we call determination when it is considered under the attribute of extension and deduced from the laws of motion and rest." For the sake of brevity, let me just say that whereas Spinoza did not have too much to say about how this translates into a community-based world, that was not the case with Kant. The equilibrium between body and soul is key to his understanding of "the social" to which the individual belongs.[1]

Our electronic shadow is the historically determined *culmination* of Being; furthermore, it cannot go. For this reason, the issue raised here is not a question of technology as such but of ontology.

Chapter 1

To be more precise: each of us as an individual has only a vague and quite undeveloped sense of our global presence compared to our usual sense-of-Self. The difference is an illusion, because the sense-of-Self is obviously an artifice of cognition, meaning that we have just as little chance of understanding our supposed sense-of-Self as our global presence, despite the promises of the Enlightenment. Nonetheless, as a practical matter, our individual sense-of-global is simply too defused when compared to the evolutionarily produced and culturally reinforced narcissism of the

1. Benedictus de Spinoza, *Ethics,* ed. E. M. Curley (1677; repr., London: Penguin Books, 1996), 73; Spinoza, *Opera,* ed. Carl Gebhardt, vol. 2 (1677; repr., Heidelberg: C. Winter, 1972), 144.

autonomy of Self to become the foundation of speculation, for the simple reason that there is no obvious place to begin to understand that relationship, conceptually, historically, or cognitively. But when we accumulate all the individual "globals" at the scale of billions of people, we arrive at a Global-as-abstraction that allows us to more effectively theorize the balance between Being and Global and the illusory promises and compulsions that *both* impose of the Self. That is what is implied by the word *Being-Global*.

We might imagine the Global as a peripherality to Being, as a technical–civilizational extension of the primacy of Self, but that would be wrong. We must start from the premise that ontology and globality are continually exchanging position between center and periphery.

The Indian government recently set up a system called the Unique Identification Authority of India, the objective of which is to collect the biometric and demographic data of residents, store them in a centralized database, and issue a twelve-digit unique identity number called Aadhaar to each citizen. It is thought to be the largest such project in the world, though other governments have different ways of collecting this information. There are restrictions on how Aadhaar can be used; nonetheless, the government can use it to track the movements, phones, and monetary transactions of suspected terrorists. The more terrorists, the more leeway, meaning of course that Aadhaar can monitor the activities of anyone. In this, India is simply playing catch-up to the other large nation-states. And it is of course not just nation-states that desire and possess the capacity to produce biometric information banks.

Chapter 2

As to the issue of civilianization, I am referring to a historical arc that begins roughly with the Fourth Geneva Convention (1949), the aim of which was to set forth protocols that could save lives during wartime. The implicit hypothesis was that after hostilities had ceased, civilians were to be the essential components of a return to normalcy. Military conflict represented disruption, whereas the civilian world represented continuity. This idea of a *civilian* challenged the traditional, nineteenth-century notion of a *citizen*. Whereas a citizen was by definition a citizen of a nation, a civilian, as a noncombatant, was seen in more open-ended and precarious legal terms. I am arguing that there has been an *implicit* expansion of its definition. Because the data world of today is in essence a world of *militarized* data—data as a value that has to be protected and defended—we become de facto civilians in the looser sense of that word. Legally, I am a citizen of the United States, but through my involvement, unwilling or not, with data deities, whose reach is global, I become part of a new civilian world that has normalized military technology and accepts the fact that these deities have become military entities unto themselves.

There has been a good deal of discussion about artificial life software or reconfigurable and evolvable hardware. While this is part of my argument, I am instead talking about how we as humans naturalize even unalive technologies into our life cycles.

The arguments that technology is "neither good nor bad," or that it is the proverbial "tool," are common fallacies that one encounters in the technoliterature. Technology is both good *and* bad. But how we determine what is good and what is bad is violently unstable both in time and in space.

I am separating the discussion of ontology from the question of what a human is. The mistake is often to combine the two and thus to use ontology to modify the Human. Ontology, as I see it, is a *descriptive* process—a question, one can say, of modeling, which is why algorithms are so important, if not essential, to the conversation. A discussion on the issue of the Human, by way of contrast, almost always begs the issues of improvement and of the relationship between self-transformation and the transformation of others from the perspective of ethics and morality (self-policing and the policing—implied or overt—of others). The one can lead to the other but cannot *be* the other. What I am thus proposing here is a type of natural history of post-ontology.

Chapter 3

The world of global algorithms has profoundly changed what it means to be global. As an indication of just how rapidly this has happened, one need only look at *The Global Age* by Martin Albrow (1996). The word "computer" does not appear once, a mistake that no contemporary scholar will repeat. Or so one would think. Jan Nederveen Pieterse's book *Globalization and Culture* (2009) also makes no mention of computation. The assumption is that the computerized world is just there, operating smoothly at the behest of corporations.

There is a tendency among some critics to assume that the electronic age is an age of Nowness that produces a flow into which we are expected to release ourselves to the strange world that opens up for us in this hypermodern era. Such a psychologically based argument can easily fall victim to the seductions of what is meant by the idea of the Electronic and thus comes dangerously close to giving the electronic world an autonomous teleological mission based on the false assumption that its core agenda is speed. The data world moves not only at multiple world scales but also at vastly different temporalities and is thus designed to *not* flow, or not flow smoothly across the board. I see the friction *within* data as an end unto itself, for it is there that the Human is produced.

Chapter 4

The impossibility of ever knowing our onto-algorithmic nature places in stark relief the equal impossibility of ever getting to the ground of Being.

A Marxian position on surplus would hold that it is an instrument of production and exploitation that has to be visible in the system of economies. In the post-ontological world, the visibility of data surplus is violently repressed. Furthermore, it is continuously traumatized by the inbuilt coefficient of self-incomprehensibility and insecurity.

Being-Global is not the same thing as Being-Digital. The latter focuses on information and how it moves through space, its reception aestheticized and designed to make it compatible with human interfaces. Being digital is to live in a world of "bit radiation" that will map the positive energy of human life.[2] The key phrase is "artificial intelligence"—about machines understanding humans "with the same subtlety we can expect from other human beings."[3] Being-Global is, indeed, saturated with digitalness/digitalitis. But being digital still assumes a type of ethos of what a human/superhuman machine can do as well as that it will be replaced by, or be equivalent in intelligence and capacity to, humans. It will be

2. Nicholas Negroponte, *Being Digital* (New York: Knopf, 1995), 56.
3. Ibid., 165.

smarter, perhaps, and do things more efficiently. Being-Global is not sure where and what is meant by "artificial." Being-Global is also not sure where and what is meant by "intelligence"—another onto-centric word of the modernists. The boundary between artificial and nature is unknowable. Why even worry about it? The main problem, therefore, of theorizing from the perspective of "artificial intelligence" is that it assumes that the scientific-engineering goal as understood by computer experts and computer theorists is how computers actually work. After all, they should know. But the reality is that they are the least likely to be able to grapple with the purposefully constructed, geo-political-theological frictional/devotional realities that exist in the zone of interaction between the proverbial human and the proverbial computer.

Defenders of the digital age will point out that the old-fashioned, binary distinction between author and audience is now obsolete and that, as a result, organizations can promote events and activities around multiple users, digital networks with open access, and participatory processes, all of which can certainly revolutionize our understanding of politics, cities, and architecture.[4] However, the discourse of optimism is starkly offset by the brutal realities that have all too quickly synthesized themselves into what we call modern life. Each iPhone requires two hundred pounds of mined material. At the very moment when we, as a global community, finally accept the dangers of car emissions, we are blissfully repressing the ecological disasters of a different making. As the Industrial Age of polluting machines has become roboticized, the new so-called Digital Age will frack the earth into oblivion, producing in the process a two-tiered world of wealth and poverty. All civilizational regimes since the beginning of "civilization" see exploitation as an instrument of legitimate authority.

Eric Schmidt and Jared Cohen are the authors of *The New Digital Age: Transforming Nations, Businesses, and Our Lives* (2013). As Google executives, they end on the upbeat note that sooner or later. the digital age will work out for the best to "create a new world of possibilities." Naturally, "choices matter." "It is not going to be easy," "parents will need to talk about this with

---

4. See Carlo Ratti and Matthew Claudel, *Open Source Architecture* (New York: Thames and Hudson, 2015).

their children," "there is no quick fix," and so forth. From a pro-business, political-technical point of view, it makes sense to keep the spin a positive one, but from a philosophical point of view, it gets us nowhere.

I disagree with Peter Sloterdijk's claim that the history of global capitalism spanned the era from 1942 to 1945 and that, after World War II, we have little more than just a "froth" of interconnections.[5] His view is grounded on the standard idea of capitalism as a singular concept driven by its place and destiny in world history. In essence, it is a Hegelianist position. The word "computer" does not even appear in the index! Sloterdijk's claims are also offset by a thesis that sees capitalism as a release of the subject from constraints. Capitalism "erodes convictions, monisms and forms of rugged primalness, replacing them with the awareness that possible choices and side exists are available at all times."[6] This is little more than a post-Enlightenment cliché. What is missed is not only that this fleshing out of the subject has produced a new type of human, a Human+, but that it comes at a huge cost for capitalism, and not just in financial terms. The consequences of capitalism's inner (self-)torture are difficult to foretell but are hardly rosy. It is not "froth"; it is "goth."

Data capitalism is of a fundamentally different order than the capitalism of old in that the algorithmic world as promoted by capitalism has produced a level of *inter*-capitalistic violence of a new and unprecedented nature. Therefore one has to add to the traditional vertical relationship between corporation and consumer—a relationship built around ever-fallible principles like consumer trust and brand loyalty—a horizontal relationship where corporations fight against a whole host of actors, from governments and hackers to other corporations. The humanizing of the former with rather important geopolitical implications obscures from view the (in)humanizing of the latter. This returns to my theme that corporations are not "people," as the U.S. legal system claims, but demi-gods, locked in mythical and violent struggles for survival and supremacy.

5. Peter Sloterdijk, *In the World Interior of Capital: For a Philosophical Theory of Globalization,* trans. Wieland Hoban (Malden, Mass.: Polity Press, 2013), 157.

6. Ibid., 210.

For an excellent description of what a digital anthropology would be, see Tom Boellstorff's essay "Rethinking Digital Anthropology."[7] Generally speaking, however, digital anthropology studies the online realities as they stand in admittedly ambiguous contrast with offline realities. Post-ontology starts from the presumption that we are always online, and not just individually, but as a global population.

One could, of course, hope that a good map of our social/digital ecology would help us see the otherwise invisible power relations. This is the approach of actor-network theory (ANT), as understood by Bruno Latour, among others, which tries to map relations between things and concepts as well as, of course, between humans and concepts. ANT sees itself as a powerful descriptive force, not as an instrument to theorize behavior. As Latour notes, explanation does not follow from description; it is description taken that much further. "Explanation emerges once the description is saturated."[8] One might wonder when the moment of "saturation" might actually be a type of false positive. The need to see if a saturation is real means that one soon winds up with the problem of the dog chasing its tail. At any rate, my interest is not in analyzing the world but in discussing ontology as a type of energy field (with human and so-called nonhuman actors at play) that is both shaped and shaping.

Chapter 5

To reduce the issue of language to marketing is to miss the entire seismic shift in our culture regarding how we understand and speak the technological. We cannot assume that language is just the accident of communication.

The core mistake of much of the literature is to assume that digital has something to do with electronic media, thus the fascination with questions around access, speed, mobility, social networks, innovation, privacy, and the like. Although these are

7. Tom Boellstorff, "Rethinking Digital Anthropology," in *Digital Anthropology* (London: Berg, 2012), 39–60.

8. Bruno Latour, "Technology Is Society Made Durable," in *A Sociology of Monsters: Essays on Power, Technology, and Domination* (London: Routledge, 1991), 129.

all real-time problems, I am focusing on the psychophilosophi-
cal nature of the algorithmic. In other words, I am interested in
the "mathematics"/"language," where both "mathematics" and
"language" have to be put in quotes so that one does not assume
that they are stable conditions. The "media" perspective will inevitably bring us no further than the old philosophical problem
of exteriority, namely, of messaging and the like. The algorithm
is not a medium, nor is it in any way "mediating," except in its
most primitive, exobiological sense. On one hand, this emerging
language is the historically determined poetics of our ontological
imaginary. On the other hand, it is the expression of the newly
haunting failure of the ontological to externalize (i.e., mediate)
its theoretically proclaimed organic unity. The English language
proved to be the right language at the right time for this phe-
nomenon.

Deontology should be understood as the attempt to evacuate
the Self to come to understand the Other, as far as that is even possible. It is an idea that speaks to a potential and not to a particular
practice. It is the necessary counter to the false assumption that
ontology can be described autonomously as a condition of Being.
In my view, deontology must remain a theoretical condition, for
it is what allows ontology to build meaningful social communities outside the orbit of its reproducible familiarity. Deontology—
as a theoretical beginning point for practice—protects us from
a Heideggerian-styled narcissism of Self. Without it, there is
only tribality or agrocivilizational, self-identitiariansim (reinforced through monotheism and/or nationalism, for example),
and all the required construction of foreignness that goes with
those worldviews. In the post-ontological world, this changes in that the I is undercut by the algorithmic universe. The I
is the object—not the subject—of the deontological effort of understanding that in essence precedes it. But this effort, though it
seems, technically at least, to come from outside, let's say, from
hackers, banks, or government agencies (forcing us to continually update and protect our "privacy"), is actually the necessary
support structure of our traditional sense-of-Self, just as, in re-
verse, that sense-of-Self is the platform on which the deontological operates. Deontology is not to be confused with deontology.
The latter word derives from the Greek word *deon-*, or "duty,"
and is thus the study of duty-based realities.

The distinction between private and public is a modern one created in the nineteenth century. To assume that privacy is some activity that can be defined, instrumentalized as information, and then protected and be therefore private is absurd

Chapter 6

We need to put aside the arrogance of abstracting the human as different from the inhuman, an arrogance bred into the separation of the two words, thus my rather simple attempt to get to a one-word concept. Placing the negative in parentheses creates other problems for sure, especially in its pronunciation. But at least the vectors are pointing in two directions simultaneously to protest against the archaic presumption that the distinction between human and inhuman is clear-cut, whether from a theoretical or moralistic point of view. My argument is that only now are we really becoming Human+, if in the form of the (in)human.

Jean-François Lyotard, in *The Inhuman* (French, 1988; English, 1991), argues that because of artificial intelligence, the human race is busy with a project that displaces that which is human from its midst.[9] Basically, he fears that computers will take over. This fear, generated as a response to technoenthusiasts, might indeed be a real one but is not at the core of my argument. We cannot assume that it is the computer that is the inhuman without some recourse to the metaphysics of the Human as a self-devotional project. It is impossible to tell where the Human and the Inhuman are to be found. It could quite well be that our algorithmic identity makes us more human than ever before. The main problem, however, is that Lyotard's interpretation of the computer is based on the standard idea that can be reduced to its binary logic. As many others and I have pointed out, algorithms are *not* aimed after some magical idea of intelligence, despite what the AI community promises, but after something called "modeling." And as I have argued more specifically, the modeling of the Human is always designed to be imperfect and incomplete; otherwise, the whole food-digestive system collapses.

9. Jean-François Lyotard, *The Inhuman: Reflections on Time* (1988; repr., Stanford, Calif.: Stanford University Press, 1991).

If the conversation about a posthuman has opened an important and timely discussion about humans as/and animals, the
post-ontological aims to open a conversation about humans as/
and packages. Just as we are packaged to be properly formatted
from the perspective of the algorithmic ether, packages in all their
tracked mobility become "like humans."

It is a little astonishing that in a book titled *Architectural
Theories of the Environment: Posthuman Territory* (2013), which
contains numerous excellent articles, the word "algorithm"
does not appear even once. As I have tried to argue, just because *technē* disappears into the biological does not mean that
it should disappear from our critique. A common mistake is to
assume that the algorithmic is a subset of the concept digital,
when in reality it is the other way around.

My psychogastronomical argument is, once again, meant to
contrast with machine-intelligence positions or those positions,
even critical to the world of data, that nonetheless begin with
the equation between data and cognition (such as N. Katherine
Hayles's argument about "cognisphere"). The important relationship is not between mind and machine, which developed
historically only because computers were made by scientists,
and we have tended to preserve their now antiquated viewpoint
in our theoretical deliberations, but between body and data,
which can then be reduced to a question of heat, the caloric, on
one hand, and thermodynamics, on the other. In comparison to a
cognisphere, I would suggest we talk of a thermosphere, which
in turn is based on a single principle: motion. Motion has to be
both natural (and continually naturalized within the realities
of language and capitalism) and induced (i.e., through "innovation").

Even though the nation-state still garners most of the press
when it comes to the world of politics, we should see the world
through a series of what many political commentators sometimes call phantom states. I expand that list to include the
Guadalajara drug cartel, Apple, Harvard University, Islamic
Caliphate, UNESCO, Egypt, and so forth. (I include Egypt because a vast part of the economy is controlled by the military,
from the manufacture of basic items such as bottled water and
furniture to infrastructure, energy, and technology projects.
"We're dealing with a brand new economy that's now run by

'Military Inc.'"[10] Unlike nations in the traditional sense, which have at least some relationship to the idea of citizenship, these entities operate with freer license to pursue their self-interest and thus to exploit and manipulate data capitalism in creative ways. Given that Harvard's endowment is bigger than half of the world's economies, that the drug trade is about 1 percent of the world GDP, and that Apple's value is bigger than all but nineteen countries' GDPs, we quickly realize that if we add up the wealth of these so-called phantom entities, we are *not* really talking of phantoms. It is the nation-state that is the phantom.

In the view of Andrew Pickering, machines, instruments, facts, theories, conceptual and mathematical structures, disciplined practices, and human beings are in constantly shifting relationships with one another—"mangled" together in unforeseeable ways that are shaped by the contingencies of culture, time, and place. While this may be true, my critique is more focused on construction/dissolution of the Human in the context of an algorithmic consciousness.[11]

Chapter 7

Kant argued that human sociability leads naturally to anthropology as the study of who we are as social creatures. For him, our sociability leads us to produce things he calls categories that firm up our discussions and thoughts and that have longer life cycles than a human and thus guide us to an improved world. The post-ontological reopens the first part of that Kantian space, what we might call the Social, but today, sociability does not bear fruit in the form of stable concepts because it activates itself as a type of riff on cultural norms. But whereas a postmodernist might argue that once the heavy lid of ontology is removed, a thousand flowers can bloom, a post-ontologist knows that the situation is bipolar. The ontological and the deontological continuously modify each other, but in ways that may or may not be readily apparent at any

10. Abigail Hauslohner, "Egypt's 'Military Inc' Expands Its Control of the Economy," *The Guardian,* March 18, 2014, http://www.theguardian.com /world/2014/mar/18/egypt-military-economy-power-elections.

11. Andrew Pickering, *The Mangle of Practice: Time, Agency, and Science* (Chicago: University of Chicago Press, 1995).

given time. The ontological and the deontological are almost in-commensurable, because for most people, the two are negotiated through the slippery world of metaphors and linguistic plays. Yet these linguistic plays are the very glue that holds it all together.

I am not engaging in a critique of ontology but in a critique of onto-centrism. The critique of ontology certainly dates back to before Kant and the critique of God's existence as a determinant of Being. But the separation of ontology from theology did not really solve the problem in the long run, thus the necessity of Derrida's critique of ontology, as a critique of the metaphysics of a hidden presence. Thus also his tacit acceptance that God still somehow exists. His critique of the human realm—leaving God out its realm—does little to actually remove metaphysical operations from their usual position. As I pointed out at the beginning, we need to reject the assumed primacy of monotheism, as if by speaking the word "God," we are also speaking for nonmonotheistic worldviews. My role here is not to deconstruct metaphysics but to point out that in the post-ontological world, ontology undergoes competing forces that have to be accommodated in a potential critique. One strengthens its sense of place and thus its potential identification with metaphysics of various types. The other, built around the *plurification* of metaphysical options, a structural requirement in the nonmonotheistic world in which we live, weakens the ontological grasp on the Self and renders it vulnerable to the continual radiography of data, producing frictional incongruities between medical records, police records, tax records, e-mail histories, and so forth. The problem with the Derridean critique is that for every metaphysics that it claims to identify (and then largely in the Western intellectual tradition), a thousand new ones are in reality now being born in the swirls of everyday life. The Derridean critique also assumes a remoteness from religion—but allows a quiet nod to religiosity nonetheless—that only a Eurocentric, liberalist, post-Enlightenment philosophy can sustain and thus does not account for the vast human universe of religions, religiosities, spiritualities, ancestralities, mountain cults, animisms, shamanisms, new age yoga movements, and so on, all of which are already becoming increasingly embedded in our social realm. In a post-ontological perspective, all of these are in play along with a host of new "deities," the international corporations, nation-states, and so forth that act like premonotheistic deities, which are rarely stable. To consider these corporations as deities, though clearly oddball, has the advantage that it keeps us from getting sucked into an economic-centrist discourse. It also allows us to accept a certain crisis of theological presence.

Chapter 8

I agree with Deleuze when he stated, "The simulacrum is not a degraded copy. It harbors a positive power, which denies *the original and the copy, the model and the reproduction.* At least two divergent series are internalized in the simulacrum—neither can be assigned as the original, neither as the copy. . . . There is no longer any privileged point of view except that of the object common to all points of view. There is no possible hierarchy, no second, no third. . . . The same and the similar no longer have an essence except as *simulated,* that is as expressing the functioning of the simulacrum."[12] But one should not draw from this the conclusion that the difficulty of distinguishing between model and copy spells the end of the meaning of and purpose to life and philosophy or that it produces, as one commentator phrased it, a "tyrannical" reduction of subjectivity. Much to the contrary, I argue that this condition was predicted in the false attempt to differentiate the two to begin with. We have now closed the gap.

No matter how hard Deleuze tries to get us to see past the duality, and to envision the simulacrum as self-determining, he cannot help but invert the inversion and claim that it is a "false as power" that sets up the world of "consecrated anarchy," assuring that the inevitable "universal collapse" is a "positive and joyous event," a "creative chaos."[13] I think we should try to avoid the fallacy of the sublime. As I have tried to show, the continued attempt to anthro-emotionalize the image of our future returns us only again to a privileged subject position and the romanticization, if not intellectual, fetishization of loss. There is no such thing as anarchy in the post-ontological world. Anarchy may be there in places, but it is constructed in certain well-defined doses

12. Gilles Deleuze, "Plato and the Simulacrum," trans. Rosalind Krauss, *October* 27 (1983): 53.
13. Ibid.

so that the deities can perpetuate their raison d'être. The problem, as I see it, shifts from a political one—anarchy—to an agro-hallucinatory one.

Donna Haraway includes under the definition of *machine* "communication systems, texts and self-acting ergonomically designed apparatus" to undermine the narrow association of body with nature.[14] Though an important point, I argue that the post-ontological world permits us to identify with nature more so than ever. It is an illusion, of course, because nature as a concept belongs to antiquated ontological reasoning.

There is a difference between post-ontology and postmodernism. From a postmodern perspective, the loss of ontological certainty is experienced in the form of a diminished faith in met-anarratives and, simultaneously, as a return to the possibility of relevance of the body, everyday private experience, and the local community. Post-ontology might, in fact, further *enhance* the ostensible realness and relevance of the body and its experiences and thoughts. But the realness (or lack thereof) is not the issue in post-ontology. Post-ontology disassociates Being from a *judgment* about what is real and certain.

In the military context, where it was developed, *soft torture* refers to the use of environmental input (manipulation of sleep, temperature, clothing, body image, anxiety level, sense of dignity, and sense-of-Self) to bring about demoralization and to extract "actionable intelligence." Whether "good" intelligence ever emerges from such scenarios is a matter of much debate; experienced interrogators say such information is never useful. I use *soft torture* here a little differently, even though its purpose is very often to produce actionable intelligence on us. The main difference is that in the post-ontological world, this soft torture does not require torturers. We willingly participate in the structuring/destructuring of our Being because we know that the torturers—our contractual deities—are themselves tortured. The deities and we exist in a distributed set of ever-changing torture relationships, responding to new conditions and new information that works on both sides of the equation.

14. Donna J. Haraway, *Simians, Cyborgs, and Women: The Reinvention of Nature* (New York: Routledge, 1991), 1.

Afterword

For narrow through their members scattered ways
Of knowing lie. And many a vile surprise
Blunts soul and keen desire. And having viewed
Their little share of life, with briefest fates,
Like smoke they are lifted up and flit away,
Believing only what each chances on,
Hither and thither driven; yet they boast
The larger vision of the whole and all.
But thus wise never shall these things be seen,
Never be heard by men, nor seized by mind;
And thou, since hither now withdrawn apart,
Shalt learn—no more than mortal ken may span.[15]

—WILLIAM ELLERY LEONARD, excerpt from *The Fragments of Empedocles*

How could they know, how could they know
What I've been thinking?
But they're right inside my head because they know
Because they know, what I've been hidin'[16]

—BIG DATA, "Dangerous," featuring vocalist Daniel Armbruster of Joywave

15. William Ellery Leonard, *The Fragments of Empedocles* (Chicago: Open Court, 1908), 15–16.

16. Big Data, "Dangerous," featuring Joywave, SoundCloud, https://soundcloud.com/bigdatabigdata/big-data-dangerous.

Dates

Some critical dates in the formation of post-ontological consciousness follow:

1963: Syncom 2 launched

Late 1960s: Delphi method developed by RAND

1968: *2001: A Space Odyssey*

1971: Wiland Services

1972: First video game competition

1976: Cray-1, one of the world's first supercomputers

1977: CATIA

1977: Kmart Corporation established

1978 to circa 1986: U.S. "deregulation" period

1980: Rhinoceros 3-D

1980: Computer Bismarck—generally credited as the first "serious" computer war game

1981: Convention for the Protection of Individuals with Regard to Automatic Processing of Personal Data

1982: Sprint

1982: The 414s hack the Los Alamos Laboratories

1983: K. Pardo and Remy Landau patent granted

1983: Verizon

1984: Commercial Space Launch Act

1984: Comprehensive Crime Control Act

1985: Computational global weather implemented

1985: Media Lab established at MIT

1986: Principles of Data Mining and Knowledge Discovery (First European Conference)

1986: Computer Fraud and Abuse Act

1987: First appearance of Data in Star Trek

1988: The Morris Worm

1989: SX-3 supercomputer

1990: First Nintendo World Championships

1990: Operation Sundevil—crackdown on "illegal computer hacking activities"

1990: Red Brick Systems, founded by Ralph Kimball, introduces a database management system specifically for data warehousing

1991: World Wide Web

1990s: ThinThread (NSA)

1993: SAT-2, first Internet cable to Africa (–2013)

1994: Amazon.com

1994: MetaCrawler (one of the Web's first search engines)

1995: JavaScript

1995: Data Warehousing Institute, a for-profit organization that promotes data warehousing

1996: First major use of phishing in a data breach

1996: Telecommunications Act

1997: Bilbao Guggenheim—one of the earliest uses of CATIA in a civilianized context

1997: Pharmaceutical companies advertise to the public

1997: Philip Kennedy, a scientist and physician, designs the world's first human "cyborg," Johnny Ray

1997: Yandex

1997: Grupo ACS

1997: Priceline

1998: Google

1998: PayPal

1999: *Inside the Mind of the Shopper: The Science of Retailing*

1999: Shazam

1999: Blogger

1999: Industrial and Commercial Bank of China

1999: Open Web Application Security Project

Late 1990s: Online banking developing

2000: Global positioning open to civilian use

2000: One of the earliest Innovation Districts: 22@Barcelona Project

TRANSITION TO THE POST-ONTOLOGICAL

2000: Verizon Wireless

2000: SketchUp (formerly: Google Sketchup)

2000: ILOVEYOU worm

2000: TripAdvisor

2001: Wikipedia

2001: Expedia

2001: USA PATRIOT Act

2002: *The Rise of the Creative Class*

2002: Homeland Security Act

2003: Myspace

2004: Facebook

2004: Google Books

2005: YouTube

2005: HomeAway

2006: Twitter

2007: Beginning of the Great Recession

2009: *The Shadow Factory*

2009: Foursquare

2010: Operation Aurora (with ties to China)

2010: Kendall Square innovation district expands

2010: *Delivering Happiness: A Path to Profits, Passion, and Purpose*

2012: Instagram

2012: "Rogue algorithm" causes havoc on the New York Stock Exchange

2013: *Paranoia* (the movie)

2013: Largest known data theft in history

2013: Edward Snowden revelations

2014: Neurocore

2014: Titan, now the second-fastest supercomputer in the world

2014: Sony hacked

2015: Stick and Find (locate anything)

2015: Anthem—names, dates of birth, and other information on 78.8 million people stolen in one of the largest hacks to date

2015: PalmSecure

2015: Vault—hide your personal photos

Mark Jarzombek is a professor at MIT, where he has been teaching since 1995. He works on a range of topics in the field of the history and theory of architecture.